CRETE

guide to the i:

A complete gui
with 172 colour illust
and maps

EDITIONS
TOUBI'S ®
ΕΚΔΟΣΕΙΣ

Texts: Y. DESYPRIS, N. DRAMITINOU - ANASTASOGLOU
Photographs: T. SPYROPOULOS, Archives: M. TOUBIS

Artwork: NORA DRAMITINOU - ANASTASOGLOU
Photosetting: MARIA LIAKOU
Montage, four-colour editing, printed by: M. TOUBIS GRAPHIC ARTS, Athens -Tel. (01) 9923874

Copyright © 1996 EDITIONS MICHALIS TOUBIS S.A.
519 Vouliagmenis Ave.,Ilioupoli 16 341 - Tel. (01) 9923876, Fax: (01) 9923867

ISBN: 960 - 7504 - 29 -1

Good is this earth, we're fond ot it, like the curly bunch of grapes
in the dark blue air, my God, how it hangs there, shaking in the gale.
And it's pecked by the spirits and the birds of the wind;
let us peck at it too and so refresh our mind!

from the Odyssey A Modern Sequel
by Nikos Kazantzakis

Millions of years ago Aegeis, the dry land that joined Greece to Asia Minor, sank into the Mediterranean Sea and only the peaks of its mountains were left above the surface. These events gave birth to Crete, that large island with its high mountains and rare beauty. Its famed gorges, sheer coastal cliffs and strange plateaus, which seem like dry lakes, and its large, dazzling white sand beaches are the remains of this awesome cosmogony which created the island, but are also the magnet which attracts visitors all these years later.

It is not only its natural beauties that are of interest. There are also the
antiquities of Crete. Ancient Minoan civilization with its palaces.
The civilization that arose 4,000 years ago and lasted for over
a thousand years on the island. It is even the Cretan Soul, unruly
and courageous, that so much has been said about.
You become so attached to these people, so proud and so hospitable,
that you want to go back again and again, from your very first visit,
as if Crete were your second home.

NATURE & LAND
Location & Climate - Mountains -
Morphology - Products -

MYTHOLOGY
Zeus - Europa -
Minotaur - Theseus -

HISTORY
From the Neolithic period

MINOAN CIVILIZATION
Religion - Bull-fighting (Bull-dancing)
Architecture - Painting -
Gold work - Stone carving -

CIVILIZATION & TRADITION
Manners - Customs - Occupations -
Dance - Music - Songs -Literature -
Icon Painting (Cretan School) -

INFORMATION - INDEX

THE TOUR

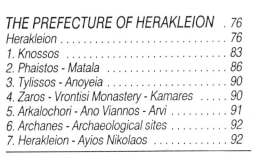

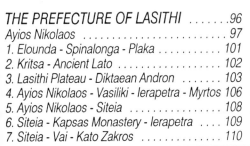

NATURE & LAND
Location - Climate - Mountains - Morphology - Products - Flora - Fauna

Crete lies in the eastern Mediterranean basin and it is the Mediterranean's fifth largest island (after Sicily, Sardinia, Cyprus and Corsica). Together with the islets off its shores, Crete has a total area of 8,335 square kilometres and according to the 1981 census it has a population of 500,000. It is surrounded by three continents, lying about 100 kilometres from Europe, 180 from Asia and 270 from Africa.

Its position, together with the morphology of the terrain, guarantees Crete a Mediterranean climate which is among the mildest in Europe.

The island is set between the Cretan, Ionian and Libyan Seas. The water reaches great depths around its coasts, sometimes exceeding 3,000 metres. The coastline of Crete has a total length of 1,046.4 km., and consists of sandy beaches, picturesque coves and little harbours, and steep cliffs.

The island is largely mountainous and is crossed, from west to east, by the massifs of the White Mountains (2,452 m.), Mt. Ida or Psiloritis (2,456 m.), Mt. Dikti (2,155 m.) and other, lower, mountains. In former times, the greater part of these mountains was covered by dense forest.

Today, there are only two forests left: Rouva on the southern slopes of Mt. Ida and Selekano on the southern slopes of Mt. Dikti. At Vai, on the eastern extremity of Crete, is a unique forest of palm trees. As a result of the morphology of the terrain, Crete has a large variety of imposing ravines and attractive plateaus, not to mention numerous caves of historical and geological interest.

At many points on the island there are springs which feed streams and rivers. Crete's only lake lies at Kourna in the Prefecture of Chania and covers an area of approximately 60 hectares.

The plains which are formed between the mountains are relatively fertile, and this is particularly true of those which lie along the southern coasts (the largest is Messara, which is 50 km. long and 7 km. wide).

These marked climatic and geophysical differences assure Crete of an unusual range of products all the year round. The soil is very fertile and Cretan produce has been famous for its quality and taste since ancient times. Nearly 1/3 of the surface area of the island is under cultivation, and the crops include olives, citrus fruit, grapes (from which superb wine is made), chestnuts, cherries, almonds and early vegetables. Cheese and aromatic honey are also produced. In relation to Greece as a whole, Crete produces almost half the country's olive oil, most of its sultanas and large quantities of wine, fruit and vegetables.

The "Gates"
in the unique Samaria Gorge.

Indigenous Cretan plants.
1. Dittany, 2. Lily, 3. Iris, 4. Cyclamen.

The peculiar geographical position of Crete and the variety of its terrain have assured the island of a vast range of flowers and plants. Apart from the generally familiar Mediterranean flora, there are 130 species of wild flower and herb which are unique to Crete. One of these is dittany, a herb known for its medicinal properties since ancient times. Aristotle wrote that the Cretan wild goats, when injured, would eat dittany to heal their wounds. Even today, women take it during pregnancy to ease labour. All the herbs which were known to the ancient physicians can still be found today, growing on the same hills, on the same slopes, in the same ravines.
There is also variety in the fauna of the island.

Here, once more, Crete has a unique species: the ibex or wild goat, known on the island as the "agrimi". Today its population is protected. There are also deer of various sizes (the hunting of which is strictly prohibited), hares, partridges, wild pigeons, snipe and other game. The seas around the island are a marvellous playground for divers and also contain substantial populations of many types of fish.

Faience wild goat from the Minoan period, Knossos 1600 B.C. Archaeological Museum Herakleion.

Ibexes in the Samaria Gorge.

MYTHOLOGY

Zeus - Europa - Minotaur - Theseus - Daedalus - Icarus

The mythology of Crete is associated with the birth of Zeus, first among of the Olympian gods, who was called "the Cretan-born", and with Europa, daughter of an Asian king, who gave her name to our continent.

Far back in the infancy of the world, the universe was ruled by Uranus; his wife was called Gaea and his son Kronos. Kronos overthrew his father and, in order to disprove a prophecy in which he had been told that he would be displaced by his son, he swallowed his children immediately after their birth.

But when Rhea, his wife, was pregnant with her last child, Zeus, she called on Uranus and Gaea for help. They decided together that Zeus would come into the world in the Diktaean Cave. To trick Kronos, Rhea gave him a swaddled stone to swallow.

Zeus was nourished on the milk of the goat Amaltheia, whom he later rewarded by marking her horn a symbol of plenty and by transforming her into a constellation of stars. The baby was protected by brave warriors, the Kouretes, who beat their spears upon their shields to drown out the cries of the infant and prevent Kronos from hearing them. When Kronos learned of this deception, he punished the Kouretes by turning them into lions, a punishment which Zeus later mitigated by making the lion king of the animals.

When Zeus eventually managed to wrest power from his father he embarked on a series of turbulent love affairs. One of these began when his attention was drawn by the innocence and grace of Europa, daughter of King Aginora or Phoenix of Syria.

The birth of Zeus from a manuscript map, (Paris, National Library).

The abduction of Europa, coloured print by the engraver K. Grammatopoulos (National Gallery).

Zeus transformed into a bull, and Europa (Krater 450 B.C.)

He promised that afterwards he would sacrifice the bull to Poseidon. However, Minos broke his promise and kept the handsome bull (which he put out into his meadows to graze), sacrificing an ordinary bull in its place. To punish him, Poseidon caused Minos's wife Pasiphae to become infatuated with the bull. In order to satisfy her passion, Pasiphae managed with the help of Daedalus, the greatest inventor of antiquity, to hide herself inside an artificial cow and thus have intercourse with the animal. Of their union was born the Minotaur, a monster with a bull's head and the body of a man.

In order to approach the girl without being found out by Hera, his wife, Zeus transformed himself into a bull and made his appearance close to Europa and her maidens. Europa was the first of the group to pluck up the courage to approach the handsome bull; while her friends decked the animal with garlands, she mounted its back. Zeus then set off at full tilt, crossed the sea and arrived in Crete. While living with Europa there, he gave her three sons: Minos, Rhadamanthys and Sarpedon.

Minos married Pasiphae, daughter of Helios and the nymph Crete, who gave her name to the island. Minos —a semi-historical figure as well as part mythical— was a wise legislator who organised his state and was chief priest of the Minoan religion. He managed to unite at least one hundred different cities on the island, and governed them —and areas outside Crete— from his capital Knossos.

In order to win the throne of Crete, Minos asked Poseidon to lend him a bull to prove to the Cretans —and to his brothers— that he was the man chosen by the gods to succeed their king.

A Minotaur disign engraved on a coin.

On Minos' orders, Daedalus built the Labyrinth to house the Minotaur. Every year, the Athenians sent seven youths and seven maidens to be sacrificed in this complex building to the Minotaur and its lust for human flesh.

Minos had laid siege to Athens to avenge the death of his son Androgeos, who had been victorious at the Panathenaic Games and had then been killed either by those with whom he was travelling, or by the wild bull of Marathon. Zeus aided Minos by sending down a plague on the city. In their desperation to put an end to hostilities, the Athenians agreed to send the human tribute to the Minotaur each year.

The death of the Minotaur. Ret-figured kylix from the 5th century B.C. (British Museum).

It was Theseus, son of King Aigeus of Athens, who rid the Athenians of the tribute to the Minotaur, with the help of Ariadne, one of Minos' daughters, who had fallen in love with him. Ariadne gave Theseus a ball of string – 'Ariadne's thread' – one end of which he tied to the entrance of the Labyrinth. Thus no matter how far he penetrated into its depths, he would always be able to find his way out again. The Athenian hero fought the Minotaur and killed it.

Then he secretly sailed away, taking Ariadne with him as he had promised. On the way back to Athens, they stopped at Naxos, and Theseus left Ariadne there on the instructions of the goddess Athena. According to another version of the story, the god Dionysus fell in love with her and stole her from Theseus.

The point of the Minotaur story is that it demonstrates the power of Minoan Crete and the subjugation of Athens to it. To punish Daedalus for helping Queen Pasiphae, Minos locked

Daedalus and Icarus.

him and his son Icarus up in the Labyrinth. Daedalus was unable to bear the imprisonment and made wax wings for himself and his son so that they could fly out. But the feat led to a tragic end for one of these first airmen: Icarus disobeyed his father's orders and flew too close to the sun, where his wings melted. Icarus fell into the sea and was drowned; the area into which he plunged has since been called the Icarian Sea.

Theseus killing the Minotaur.
(Black-figured amphora, Paris, Louvre)

HISTORY

From the Neolithic period
to the Battle of Crete

Neolithic Period

Human beings appeared for the first time on Crete during the Neolithic period, the beginning of which is placed between 6000 and 5000 B.C., and the end around 2600 B.C.

Minoan Period

The beginning of the Minoan period coincides with the beginning of the Bronze Age.
The new civilization which would develop on and would come to dominate the island for 1,200 years was brought to Crete around 2600 B.C. by a people out of Asia Minor. Perhaps other people also came there from Egypt and Libya but they did not, any relationship to the races Egyptian or the Semites. It is probable that all these newly arrived people belonged to the Indo-European race. Unfortunately, we do not know what language they spoke, just as we know very little about the history of Minoan Crete in general.
The lack of knowledge, in regard to its history has been partially obviated, however, by the great wealth of finds the archaeological pick has brought to light. Due to these finds we have a fairly good idea of the achievements of Minoan civilization in art, social development and economic organization (see page 22).
From these rich finds we can separate the Minoan period into smaller periods and sub-periods.

According to Evans the division was as follows:
Early Minoan Period (2600-2100 B.C.)
Middle Minoan Period (2100-1600 B.C.)
Late Minoan Period (1600-1100 B.C.)
Later Professor N. Platon introduced a new dating system with new names for the periods:
The Prepalatial Period (2600-2000 B.C.)
The Old Palace Period (2000-1700 B.C.)

"Horse parade", stone sculpture from the Prinias temple (650 B.C., Archaeological Museum Herakleion). "A brilliant prelude to the history of Greek art" (M. Andronikos).

The New Palace Period (1700-1400 B.C.)
The Postpalatial Period (1400-1100 B.C.)
The latter chronological divisions also take into the account the following important dates for the evolution of Minoan civilication.
2600 B.C. The arrival of new people on Crete who brought with them a knowledge of how to work copper.
2000 B.C. The erection of the first large Minoan palaces.
1700 B.C. Their destruction by a terrible earthquake and their rebuilding a few years later, more luxurious than ever.
1400 B.C. The destruction of the second palaces, probably as a result of the explosion of the volcano on Santorini which signaled the end of the Minoan world (the Achaeans appeared immediately afterward).
1100 B.C. The conquest of Crete by the Dorians.

Reconstruction of the West wing facing the Cnetral Court of the Palace of Knossos.

From the Dorians to the Romans

Practically from the beginning of the period (1100 B.C.) an important change was noted in art. The designs on pottery changed and for the first time iron appeared as a metal used in metallurgy. Later, in the **Geometric** period (900-725 B.C.) art flourished, especially pottery. Finally, during the **Archaic period** (650-500 B.C.), a new style, called the Dedalic, made its presence strongly felt in pottery.

The Roman Period

The Romans under Metellus occupied Crete in 68 B.C. after bitter battles. Crete became a Roman province to which Cyrenaica was .also subject, with its capital at Gortyn.
This Cretan town as well as Kissamos (Kastelli) flourished during that period. Christianity appeared on Crete with the arrival of the Apostle Paul (63-66 A.D.).

The laws of Gortyn.

Byzantium (330-1204/10 A.D.)

Crete experienced Byzantine rule in two periods: the first of these (330-826 A.D.) was interrupted by the Arabs occupation (826-961), which was followed by the second Byzantine period (961-1204/10).

It was during the first Byzantine period that Christianity spread to the island and established itself. During the Early Christian period (5th-6th centuries), fine churches were built.
Crete frequently suffered from Arab raids. In 823, the Saracens conquered the island and laid siege to Herakleion, digging a moat all the way round the town. Under the rule of the Arabs, there was much persecution of Christianity and the religion's hold over the island slackened. In was not until 961 that the Byzantine general Nicephorus Phocas was able to liberate Crete and bring it back into the Byzantine Empire.
Crete returned to Byzantium (second Byzantine period) and Christianity gained in strength. It was at this time that Herakleion became the seat of the Archibishop,and churches and monasteries sprang up everywhere.

The Venetian Occupation

Venetians, after a war with the Genoans, prevailed and became the masters of the island in 1212.
The Venetian period, which would last for over 400 years, held new tribulations in store for the Cretan people who would react by revolting against their conquerors. In the end, however, these struggles would not prevent a Renaissance from occurring on the island.

The Turkish Occupation

This was the worst period for the Cretans. The Turks first occupied Chania in 1645 and then moved east destroying and burning whatever lay in their path. The great obstacle for them was the fortress at Chandax. It took a seige of 23 years to capture it. But after that they ruled the

The Byzantine chapel of St. Paul,
east of Ayia Roumeli.

island alone and the Cretans would hence-
forth live in abject slavery. Their churches
would be transformed into mosques and
their property would be confiscated.

The Cretans reacted violently to all this and
there were frequent uprisings and revolts,
the most important ones in 1770 (Daskalo-
yiannis), 1821, 1866 (the holocaust at
Arkadi) and 1897.

Liberation and Union with Greece

The holocaust at Arkadi and the bravery of
the Cretans stirred public opinion
throughout the world. Four of the Great
Powers of the time (Great Britain, France,
Russia and Italy) intervened, the Turks
were driven from the island and a "High
Commissioner" was appointed, Prince
George of Greece, who arrived in the
island at the end of 1898 to administer the
"Cretan Republic" as the now independent
state was called. Another revolt would be
needed to achieve union with Greece. That
would be the one instigated by Eleftherios
Venizelos in 1905 at Therisos. Union would
become a reality eight years later in 1913
when Venizelos had already become
Prime Minister of Greece.

The Battle of Crete (1941)

Another brilliant page was to be added to
the history of Crete. This was the great
battle the allies of Greece, along with the
population of Crete, waged against Hitler's
paratroopers in May 1941. This was to be
a part of the Cretan people's fierce
resistance during the German occupation.
The reprisals the Cretans would suffer at
the hands of their conquerors were harsh.
Whole villages were levelled and their male
inhabitants executed en masse. But the
Cretan soul did not falter because it was
well-versed in struggle and sacrifice after
so many years.

Crete under the symbol of Venice,
in a copperplate by Boschini.

21

MINOAN CIVILIZATION
(2600 B.C. - 1100 B.C.)

Religion - Bull-fighting (Bull-dancing) - Architecture - Painting - Gold work - Stone carving - Pottery

Even though we cannot be sure that these colonists introduced metalworking into Crete, there is no doubt that the Bronze Age began there around the year 2600 B.C. This was the beginning of the culture which has come to be called "Minoan civilization". The name, from Minos, the mythical king of Crete, was first used by the archaeologist Arthur Evans. The Minoan epoch is broken down into three periods: Early Minoan, Middle Minoan and Late Minoan. The first palaces were built in Crete around the start of the Middle Minoan period, that is, around 2000 B.C. Economic and political power seems to have centred on the palaces at Knossos, Phaistos, Mallia, Archanes, Zakros and Kydonia. An earthquake which shook the whole island and was followed by extensive fires seems to have destroyed the palaces around 1700 B.C. Immediately after the disaster the palaces were rebuilt even larger and more magnificent than before, and the period from 1700 B.C. to 1400 B.C. is often called The New Palace Period.

Mallia, Zakros, Phaistos and above all Knossos were at the height of their power during this period. At about this time, the ruler of Knossos seems to have expanded his kingdom to include control of Phaistos. Knossos, with its favourable geographical position in the centre of the island, was able to unite the entire island, building a network

The disc of Phaistos.

of good roads and controlling economic and political life. The size and the refined luxury of the Knossos palace are indications that this was the seat of power. Excavations have revealed that more than one script was in use in Crete at this time: a hieroglyphic script (of which the Phaistos Disc is an example) and a syllabic script, known as Linear A. Linear A has not yet been deciphered. Around 1400 B.C. there was a tremendous natural disaster which heralded the end of the Minoan culture. Earthquakes and fires destroyed Knossos and the other palaces, and the towns were emptied.

The catastrophe may have been from the eruption of the volcano on Santorini.

The calamity, however, may have been accompanied by foreigners invading Crete. At Knossos was found a section of the palace archives wreitten in Linear B script, which is identical to the writing found in Mycenean palaces.

However, the disaster in 1400 B.C. was not the absolute end of Minoan culture in Crete.

For some centuries −down to 1100 B.C.− it struggled on even though the island was under the domination of the Achaeans.

Nonetheless, it was unable to regain the brilliance of its past prosperity.

Religion in Minoan Crete

The Minoan religion strongly influenced that of the Greeks who followed, and in whose mythology Crete plays an important part. Figurines of the Great Goddess have survived from the crowning period of Minoan art, together with pictorial representations of religious ceremonies, utensils used during these ceremonies and depictions of the sacred symbols: the pair of horns, the double axe, the sacred knot, the octagonal shield, the sacred tree and so on.

The female figure occupies a central position, and we can be certain that the sacredness of fertility and eternal life was worshipped.

Bull's head. Rhyton from Knossos, 1500 B.C.

From the very inception of their culture the Cretans believed in some sort of life after death. The dead were accompanied with pots of foodstuffs and the utensils of daily life, for use not only on the journey to the next world but until the body had disintegrated entirely. The deities of Minoan Crete were worshipped not only within of the palaces but also out of doors, in natural sanctuaries, in caves and on mountain peaks. The cult of the bull and the festivals held in its honour —attended by thousands of spectators— were the nucleus of the Minoan religion.

The snake goddess (Knossos, 1600 B.C.).

Bull-dancing

Bull-fighting, or rather bull-leaping, was the most important of these ceremonies and was held in the spring, when nature and man are reborn. They were based on the sancity of the bull and on its relationship to fertility.

The bull-dancing or bull-leaping seems to have been the Minoan's favourite sport, too. The event was held in an arena in the palace and attracted enthusiastic crowds. The bull was sacrificed later, but was never killed during the leaping itself. The bull would rush snorting into the enclosed area; young boys and girls nearly naked ①, would skip out of

Bull-leaping (bull-dancing) in a Knossos wall painting, 1500 B.C.

its way, grasp its horns and vault neatly upwards, their bodies reaching high into the air ②.
As they flew through the air, they would twist so as to land gracefully on the back of the enraged animal; ③ and from there it was easy to somersault off into the arms of a waiting companion ④.

Minoan Art

To judge by their art, the Minoans must have loved nature, elegance and beauty. The works of art they produced are generally on a small scale. Painting seems to have been their chief passion, and all their murals are dominated by the element of movement, which is rendered with delicacy and vitality. The spiral was the central decorative motif. The Late Minoan period was the golden age

Their dresses were very low-cut (in effect, they went topless) and were, pulled tight at the waist, low-hanging.

The women of Minoan Crete would seem to have been emancipated: the murals show them attending religious ceremonies, dancing and sporting events in complete equality with the men. The murals, and the skeletons which have been found in caves, show the Minoans to have been short, slim and quick-footed. They were certainly fond of a good time

The stone sarcophagus of Ayia Triada with religious depictions, 1400 B.C. (Herakleion Museum).

of Minoan art, lasting approximately one hundred years. Depictions in painting and sculpture give us some idea of what the Minoans must have looked like. It would seem that the men dressed in very light clothing: they wore only a piece of multi-coloured cloth round the waist. However, we also have pictures of officials wearing lavish cloaks and head-dresses. Tight belts accentuated the narrow waists of men and women alike. The women of Crete, delicate and light-footed as we can see in the murals, took great care over dressing their hair, which they then adorned with jewels and multi-coloured ribbons.

and had very little interest in the art of war. In fact, war and hunting scenes are completely absent from Minoan art, and with the exception of stoats, wild cats, polecats and ibexes (which have survived to the present day) there do not seem to have been any wild animals on the island. Of the greatest interest are the small plaques which have been found and which must have decorated a wooden chest: they show the houses of a typical Minoan city and tell us that the Minoans lived in multi-storey buildings whose tall windows were flanked by geometrical designs.

Architecture

The Minoan palaces: In the memory of the Greeks thousands of years afterwards, the Minoan palaces assumed mythical dimensions; they were constructed with outstanding artistic skill and arranged in a labyrinthine manner.

The excavations at Phaistos, Mallia and Zakros — but above all at Knossos — have shown us exactly what those palaces looked like. The first thing that strikes one is the complete absence of walls or fortifications of any kind.

Along general lines, the palaces rather resemble each other, the main features being their inner courtyards around which were the rooms for rituals and official ceremonies.

The reconstructed north entrance to the north side of the central court of the palace of Knossos.

Painting

The interior decoration of the palaces was particularly impressive, with outstanding wall paintings. These murals were painted straight on to wet plaster (the fresco technique), presumably after a preliminary design had been made and the artist had to work fast and accurately. Perhaps this accounts for the vividness of the figures. These Minoan frescoes are a wonderful and brightly-coloured chronicle of life especially as it was lived in the palace: religious ceremonies, bull-leaping, scenes from everyday life, acrobats, bulls and wrestlers. Sometimes we are shown people seated in tiers to watch the events in a stadium, and we can see the women chatting together. Apart from the scenes of everyday life, many of the frescoes from Minoan Crete show landscapes and activities at sea, such as the famous "Dolphin" fresco.

Section of the wall painting depicting the beautiful priestess, the famous "La Parisienne", Knossos 1500 B.C.

"The Ladies in Blue", wall painting from the Knossos.

Stone carving, gold

Apart from the frescoes, we can also see wonderful work with a marked tendency towards the faithful depiction of reality in the Minoan carvings on stone, ivory and precious stones.

The miniature work of the Minoan artists reached very advanced levels, as can be seen in the jewellery and other products turned out by the island's craftsmen. Thoughout the centuries of the Minoan culture, these artists were great masters in working stone. Countless seal-stones, which served completely practical purposes, have survived to be admired today.

Gold jewellery from Mallia, 2000 B.C.

Pottery

The love of the Cretan artists for colour can also be seen in their pottery. The types of pottery which are most common in Early Minoan Crete are the rhyton, the hydria and the long-stemmed goblet. Many of these works take their names from the places where they were found. Most of them are painted in red against a background of a light shade of clay, while others have linear designs in light colours against a dark background.

The delicate Kamares ware pottery was so popular in its time that the Minoans exported it to the rest of the Mediterranean. The superb crystal vases are of a later date.

The figurines of deities, such as the goddess with the snakes, and the vases with decoration in relief showing scenes from daily life, such as that so-called the "Cup of the Report", the Harvester vase and the rhyton with representations of athletes in four bands, are all of a later date.

Sealstone made of a semiprecious stone.

Clay krater in Kamares style
(Phaistos 1800 B.C.).

CIVILIZATION & TRADITION

Manners - Customs - Occupations - Dance - Music - Songs - Literature - Icon Painting (Cretan School) - Architecture

The southernmost part of Greece, Crete lies at the crossroads of three continents. Its crucial, strategic position has been the cause of many wars on the island.

But the wars and the long years of slavery did not make it yield and the Cretans have proudly kept all the manners and customs they have had for centuries. One sees this if one happens to attend a traditional Cretan wedding or some other celebration. One can enjoy the Cretan lyra and the stalwart dances and admire the dashing young men and slender young women in their traditional costumes. Wars and occupations were not able to prevent the intellectual and artistic flowering of the island. We are not speaking of the marvellous achievements of Minoan civilization here for they occurred during a time of peace. We are speaking of many years later. When the Byzantine churches on Crete were built and their wonderful icons painted (14th century). The period when painting flourished and particularly the icon painting of the famous Cretan School (16th century) followed by the appearance of the great Cretan painter Domenicos Theotokopoulos, known as El Greco. When the works of Georgios Chortatzis and Vitcenzios Kornaros were played in the theaters (17th century). We are even speaking of the recent past, of that great Cretan writer Nikos Kazantzakis.

As in the past, so today, the Cretans continue to be employed at farming and animal husbandry. The main products of the island are olive oil, wine, the famous raki (tsikoudia), grapes, citrus fruit and cheese and the equally large output of early fruits and vegetables. Among its other products mention should be made of folk arts and crafts especially the weavings, embroideries, portable icons, ceramics and silver and gold accessories.

Fabric with a motif taken
from a wedding procession.

Cretan tradition is still very much alive on the island. But to find it, one has to travel inland, to the slopes of Psiloritis, the White Mountains or of Dikte. Up in those imposing mountains are villages which tourism has not touched. Here, people are different: they still live with their customs, their occupations, their habits and the beliefs of the past, and they keep their traditions alive.

The Cretans have dancing in their blood. For them, the dance is a chance to let off steam, to externalise the restlessness and dynamism of their spirits. This can be seen most clearly in the leaping dance ("pidichtos", as it is called).

The best-known Cretan dance is the "pentozalis", a very manly performance reminiscent of the "pyrrichios", the war dance of the ancient Greeks, which also used to be danced by armed Cretans. The pentozalis is danced throughout Crete. The dancers stand in a circle around the lyra-player, whose central position emphasises the fact that he gives the dance its rhythm. The music starts slowly and gradually builds up to a frenetic speed, with a leaping beat.

The "syrtos" is a little milder, but the steps of the leading dancer are, if anything, more showy than those of the pentozalis. The Cretan syrtos generally resembles the dance of the same name performed elsewhere in Greece; there are local variations, the best-known which originated in Chania.

Among other Cretan dances are the "Kastrinos" or "Maleviziotis", a fast, leaping dance, and the "sousta", which is danced by

couples. The sousta does not have the pace of the other dances, but it has all their elegance and technique.

The Cretan wedding is the social event at which dancing reigns supreme.

The Cretan wedding is the most important of all the feasts and celebrations. It combines all the crafts and daily occupations, and the Cretan traditions can here been seen in their most lively and authentic forms.

Handmade wedding bread-ring.

Anyone who gets a chance to attend a Cretan wedding should make the most of it; this is a custom whose roots lie far back in time and which has survived intact on the island. The lyra-player is an inseparable part of any group of Cretans, whether in a joyful or sorrowful mood. Without a lyra-player, there can be no festivities, and no company of friends is really complete. He is the conveyor of the musical traditions of Crete.

The traditional music of Crete is one of the most interesting elements in the folklore and art of the island. It has a very marked individual character and great variety. The basic categories into which it is divided are dance music and music to be sung to. Its goes back a long way perhaps even to ancient Greece, the Greece of the Kouretes and their dance, the pyrrichios.

There are certainly Byzantine influences in it, and at a later date the music of the whole Mediterranean had an impact.

The group of traditional instruments which accompany the dance or the song is dominated by the Cretan lyra, which can convery the spirit of Cretan music better than any other instrument.

The songs of Crete express the proud soul of the Cretan people in a simple, austere manner. They are tightly structured and highly poetic, with great imagination and a rich poetic vocabulary. These songs fall into three categories: historical songs, mantinades and rizitika.

The historical songs tell of the wars and sufferings of the Cretans.

The mantinades are rhyming couplets of fifteen-syllable lines. They are sung to simple old tunes, to the accompaniment of the lyra or a larger group of instruments, or without any accompaniment at all, because what is of importance here is the words.

The rizitika songs used to be sung only in western Crete, and particularly in the mountain villages the foofthills ("rizes") of the White Mountains and Psiloritis, from which they took their name. These are songs with many verses and no rhyme. Their themes are manliness, love, nature, hospitality, and love of freedom.

The rizitika songs of Crete are the creations of an indomitable and proud people. They are not the products of a momentary creative urge, as is the case with the mantinades, but songs which endure.

The mantinades and rizitika songs are interesting specimens of the Cretan dialect. The Cretan dialect has a very rich vocabulary which, among other features, contains more Byzantine words than any other dialect of Greece, a reminder that this island had very close links with Byzantium.

The language of Crete developed in a different manner than in the rest of Greece. In the literature of the late 16th century we can see Greek being constantly enriched with words from the Cretan dialect, which made a triumphant entry into poetry at that time. The influence of the Italian literature of the period was of decisive importance in the selection of literary genres and models. The theatre, too, was revived under Venetian influence after an interruption of some two hundred years.

In the three theatrical works by Georgios Chortatzis of Rethymno, who had studied in Padua, we can see how well the author knew the dialect of his island.

The most important figure in the poetic scene of the time, and one of the best-loved Greek authors, was Vitcenzios Kornaros (17th century). His epic entitled Erotocritos is still sung and recited everywhere today. All we know of his life is that he was from Siteia and that he probably lived in Candia (Herakleion). His work dates from the final period of Venetian rule, between 1600 and 1660.

Cretan literature became world-famous after the Second World War with the work of Nikos Kazantzakis (1883-1957). This writer's books gained particular fame in Europe and America as a result of his Alexis Zorbas, which, filmed as Zorba the Greek, was a worldwide success. Many of this novels (such as Captain Michalis, or Liberty or Death) take the struggles of the Cretans against the Turks as their theme.

The Italian influence on the arts in Crete during the period of Venetian rule was not confined to literature. It also had an impact on painting: Cretan painting consists of religious subjects recorded in portable icons and wall paintings.

When Constantinople fell to the Turks in 1453, large numbers of Greek nobles and scholars took refuge in Crete. As a result, Byzantine culture and Byzantine art took on a new lease of life. The Monastery of St Catherine in Herakleion was a particularly important centre of Byzantine culture, where theology, philosophy, music and literature were developed.

The traditional Byzantine style of painting combined with elements taken from the Italian Renaissance to form a new school of art called the "Cretan school".

The spread of the reputation of the Cretan School and of its works themselves was assisted by the commercial power of the Venetians, which was then at its height in the eastern Mediterranean. The portable icons became so valuable that their painters were able to sign simply "of Crete". Today, works by painters of the Cretan School can be seen in museums all over the world; the Ecclesiastical Museum in Herakleion has some excellent examples.

The most famous icon-painter was Theophanes (1535) a Cretan monk and painter who founded the Cretan School of painting in the 16th century; he initially worked in Herakleion but moved as far as Mount Athos, where he painted the churches of the Megiste Lavra and Stavronikita Monasteries, and Meteora, where his work can be seen in the St. Nicholas "Anapafsas" Monastery.

Among other most famous painters of this period were Michael Damaskinos, Klontzas and Ioannis Kornaros, a large icon by whom belongs to the Toplou Monastery. The youthful works of Domenicos Theotokopoulos, better known as El Greco, should also be seen as belonging to the Cretan school.

Icons are an inseparable part of the Greek Orthodox religion, and as a result they are still painted today in the traditional manner. The wood-carving in churches developed in a manner similar to the painting of icons. There are some excellent carved screens, true masterpieces.

"The Adoration of the Magi", Michael Damaskinos (16th century).
A characteristic work by the artist, one of the main representatives of the Cretan School
(Herakleion, Collection, of Ayia Aikaterini of Sinai).

Architecture

The first impressive examples of architecture on Crete were found in the excavations of the Minoan palaces (page 27).

With the spread of Christianity, and during the Byzantine period in particular, many churches were built which can still be found scattered over the island.

During the first Byzantine period numerous churches were built along the seashore which shows there was no fear of pirates.

The basilicas were large rectangular buildings which were divided internally by colonnades into three aisles. This architectural type was a development of the architectural perceptions of antiquity. Originally the churches were not just places of worship but also places for religious gatherings. The churches were decorated with marvelous floor mosaics and with paintings on the walls and ceiling.

During the second Byzantine period the Byzantines took pains to strengthen the national and religious convictions of the inhabitants. They again founded bishoprics and built an enormous number of monasteries.

Generally speaking, monastic architecture was the same for all monasteries. Built in the form of a fortress, in order to protect themselves from attack, the spaces were designed to withstand a siege. The monastery usually had an entrance in its walls, an inner courtyard with a church in the middle and cells that were a part of the fortress to economize on space.

The Arkadi Monastery from the 5th century is a representative example of the monasteries on Crete. The main church, a double-aisled basilica, is in the centre of the fortified monastery complex. The north aisle is dedicated to the Tranfiguration of Christ and the south to the Saints Constantine and Helen.

Cretan artists were able to very quickly adapt to the artistic currents of Byzantium. By the 12th century the island had acquired superb monuments.

During the Venetian period magnificent castles were built over the whole island for the fortification of the towns. The towns were also ornamented with loggias, fountains, towers and mansions. Example of this architecture still exist in the three main towns on the island, Chania, Rethymno and Herakleion.

In order to solidity their position in Crete the Venetians allowed the inhabitants to freely build and decorate their churches and monasteries. The monasteries and churches that were built during that period were influenced by the Italian Renaissance. Until the 19th century the villages of Crete were all mountainous to protect themselves from pirates and various other conquerors.

Most were shaped like an amphitheatre and followed the shape of the hill they were built on. Thus the ground floor becomes a basement to the rear and the terrace of one house becomes the veranda of the one behind. There are narrow, stone-paved lanes, courtyards with high walls and entrances made of round, hewn stones. The houses were very simple, with thick stone walls and a roof of heavy beams with clay-like earth spread over them, the well-known "doma" (flat-roof) found on the islands.

Most of the houses were two-storey with an oven outside and a fireplace inside. There was a place for the animals and storerooms on the ground floor while the owners' living spaces were on the first floor.

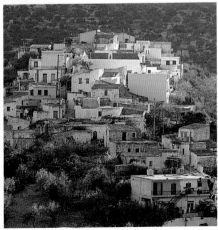

Left: The entrance to the Venetian castle of Rethymno.

Above: The triple-domed Byzantine church of the Holy Trinity Monastery of Akrotiri, Chania. Its architecture was influenced by the Renaissance.
Centre: Classical living room in a Cretan village.
Below: The village of Elounda in Lasithi.

TOURING CRETE

Your tour of Crete begins with the **Prefecture of Chania**. After visiting the sights of the impressive town of Chania itself you will head up to Cape Kydonia with its old monasteries and quiet beaches. You will take a jaunt to the village of Mournies and visit the historic Theriso after passing through the ravine there. This will be followed by the ineffable experience of going through the Samaria Gorge, never to be forgotten.

Then you will ascend to the Chrysoskalitissa Monastery and go across to Elafonissi with its amazing beaches. This is followed by Sougia with its large pebbled beach and then historic Kandanos with the market town of Palaiochora which combines the picturesque and the cosmopolitan. After getting acquainted with Kastelli Kissamos and savoring its fabulous wine, small harbour and the nearby islet of Gramvousa you will then enjoy the sunset at Falasarna with its emerald water.

You will be overwhelmed by the wild beauty of the Chora Sfakion, and get to know the Venetian Frangokastello, the authentic traditions still carried on in mountainous Anopoli and the islet of

You now enter the **Prefecture of Rehtymno**, with its Venetian town, its well-preserved castle (Fortezza) on the tip of the headland with a spacious sand beach to the east. The historic Arkadi Monastery, built on an imposing site, will deeply move you. In the Amari valley you will visit old monasteries, Byzantine churches and picturesque villages clinging to the slopes of Mt. Psiloreitis. From mountainous Spili, on the slopes of Mt. Kedros with its plentiful water, you will arrive at the bustling Ayia Galini with its small harbour, its picturesque settlement and beautiful beaches. The unique Kourtaliotiko ravine, with the lake at its exit, the palm trees lining the river banks and the crystal-clear sea will remain in your memory together with the Preveli Monastery on its imposing site and the developed coastal area of Plakias. The quaint Anoyeia, the main village on the north side of Psiloreitis, steeped in tradition, is near the Idaen Cave which according to mythology is where Zeus was raised. Finally, going along the coast from Rethymno you will reach Herakleion, a full range of hotels at your service. After going down to the picturesque bay of Bali you will visit verdant village of Fodele (in the Prefecture of Herakleion) the birthplace of the great painter Domenicos Theotokopoulos. After that, a turn-off left will take you to a tourist resort and the fabulous sand beach of Ayia Pelagia and after the extensive beach at Ammoudara you will enter the town of Herakleion.

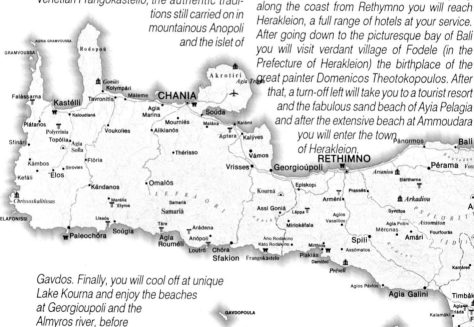

Gavdos. Finally, you will cool off at unique Lake Kourna and enjoy the beaches at Georgioupoli and the Almyros river, before arriving at Rethymno.

The Prefecture of Herakleion is the site of the large town of Herakleion, the capital of Crete. Here you will lose yourself in the rooms of the Archaeological Museum with their exhibits from Minoan civilization, unique in the world. You will be moved by the Monastery of Ayia Aikaterini and the incomparable works of the Cretan School and at the tomb of Nikos kazantzakis you will reflect on the work of that great writer. You will then visit Knossos, the most important archaeological site on Crete with the famous Palace of Minos. There is also Gortyn with its Roman antiquities, the cozy beach at Lenda, the isolated Koudoumas Monastery and the sand beaches at Kales Limnes which will precede your acquaintance with the Palace of Phaistos and the caves at Matala. This is followed by the archaeological site at Tylissos. The artificial lake at Zaros, at the base of Mt. Psiloreitis, and the remarkable Vrontisi Monastery, where Michael Damaskinos lived and painted, all the way down to the Kamares cave where the famous pottery of the same name was found are on your fourth excursion of the prefecture. This is followed by the inland excursion from Arkalochori and the mountainous Viannos down to the beach at Arvi with its banana trees. You will visit the archaeological sites at Archanes and enjoy the finest Cretan grapes.

Finally, on the coast road from Herakleion to Lasithi you will have the opportunity to get to know beautiful beachesand archaeological sites, crowned by Mallia, as well as the cosmopolitan beaches at Limena Chersonisou, Stalida and Mallia.

Your acquaintance with the Prefecture of Lasithi begins with the picturesque capital of Ayios Nikolaos itself, built on the bay of Mirabelo. The lovely resort town of Elounda and the fortress island of Spinalonga are not far off. The marvellous church of Panayia Kera (Our Lady of Kera), along with the traditional village of Kritsa and the archaeological site at Lato e Etera will create a variety of emotions in you.

This is followed by the ascent to the unique Lasith Plateau and the visit to the Diktaean Cave where, according to mythology, Zeus, the father of the gods, was born. In order go get acquainted with the town of Ierapetra on the Libyan Sea with its vast nearby beaches and its many greenhouses, your cross the narrowest point of Crete going from its northern (Pacheia Ammos) to its southern part. The route along the north coast leads you from Ayios Nikolaos to the remote and very beautiful town of Siteia. Going south from Siteia on the road to Ierapetra you will pass by ancient Praisos, the Kapsas Monastery, next to the Perivolakis ravine and the endless sand beaches all the way to Ierapetra.

Finally, from Siteia you can visit the fortress monastery of Toplou and enjoy the unique Vai with its forest of palm trees, ending your tour of the island at the fourth Minoan palace located at coastal Kato Zakros.

THE PREFECTURE OF CHANIA

It is the westernmost prefecture of Crete and to a large extent is covered by the imposing White Mountains. This majestic mountain range soars upward, lush and green, only a few kilometres from the north coast of the island to reach a height of 2,543 m., and then to descend, barren and sheer, to the Libyan Sea. Through the bowels of the earth via the Samaria Gorge. Northeast of the prefecture is Souda Bay, the largest natural harbour in Greece, the bay of Chania, and further west the Bay of Kissamos, both with huge sand beaches.

Public transport within the Prefecture is served by the KTEL buses, while caiques ply the villages of the south coast and sail out to the islet of Gavdos, the most southerly point in Europe. Chania airport, at Akrotiri (15 km. from the city) has a shuttle service to Athens and daily flights to Thessaloniki. Souda Bay, Greece's largest natural harbour, is the departure point for the daily sailings to Piraeus. There are also less frequent sailings from Kastelli Kissamou to Monemvasia, Neapoli, and Githeio in the Peloponnese, Ayia Pelagia and Kapsali on Kythera, Antikythera and elsewhere.

Chania

Chania is the second-largest town in Crete, after Herakleion, and it has a population of some 60,000. It is the capital of the prefecture of the same name and is its commercial and administrative centre. During the period of Cretan autonomy and in the first period of union with Greece, Chania was the capital of the whole island.

Chania is connected by air to Athens and by steamship (from Souda) to Piraeus.

Chania consists of the Old Town and the New Town, which blend harmoniously into an attractive, warm and friendly entity. There are old Venetian buildings – many of them now superbly restored – to take one back to the magic and glamour of an earlier age.

The Old Town is surrounded by the fine Venetian walls, dating from the 15th century, a typical example of Venetian architecture. The narrow, labyrinthine alleys with their Venetian buildings – interrupted by occasional Turkish structures – suggest something of the conquerors who came this way.

The old inner harbour, with its long Venetian pier and its lighthouse, is a reminder that Chania was once an important commercial port. Today, the old harbour is unable to meet modern requirements and ships use Souda harbour. The New Town lies around the Old, and is divided into many different quarters. This is a modern but attractive city; the streets are comfortably wide and tree-lined and every house has its garden; in the suburbs, flowers are even more predominant. It is with justice that Chania has been called the "city of flowers".

Chania stands on the site of the ancient city of Kydonia. According to the myths, the ancient city was built by Kydon, a grandson of Minos (or a son of Hermes), who was a protector of travellers: this perhaps explains the reputation of the local people for hospitality.

Archaeological investigations have shown that there was a Minoan settlement on this site. In the post-Minoan period, the powerful commercial town of Kydonia grew up in the same position and competed with the two other large cities of the period, Knossos and Gortyn. In 69 B.C., Kydonia fell to the Romans and in 325 A.D. became part of the Byzantine Empire.

Under Byzantium, the history of Chania was much the same as that of the other Cretan towns: that is, it declined. In 823 it was taken by the Arabs, who gave it the name Chania. Under the Venetians, it regained something of its former prosperity and power. In 1252, the Venetians began building the town they called "La Canea" on Kastelli hill. Nonetheless, Chania flourished as a trading centre, and at one time was called the "Venice of the East". The new walls were unable to stop the advance of the Turks, and Chania became the first Cretan city to fall to them, in 1645, after a siege of 55 days.

In 1850, Chania was declared capital of Crete. It retained this position throughout the period of Cretan autonomy (1989-1913) and even after union with Greece: in fact, Chania was the capital of Crete until 1972. During the period of autonomy, in particular, the city became very prosperous. It was the seat of the ambassadors from the Great Powers, of the High Commissioner and of the autonomous Cretan government.

Above: The lighthouse in the Venetian harbour.

Centre: The castle walls and a view of the town from the harbour.

Below: Alleyway in the Old Town of Chania.

The sights of Chania are concentrated mainly in the Old Town which is centered around the pretty Venetian harbour. At the entrance is the old Venetian lighthouse, opposite the historic Firka Fortress and the Naval Museum. Other sights are the Venetian neighbourhood of Topanas, the large walls of the Venetian fortress, built in 1540, Kastelli, the neighbourhood of Splantia with the churches of Ayios Rokkos, Ayios Nikolaos and Ayioi Anargyrioi. The Archaeological Museum is housed in the basilica of St. Francis, a Venetian church from the 14th century. This is a fine Gothic building in the style of a basilica with columns.

The Archaeological Museum collection contains interesting finds from the vicinity of Chania and Western Crete in general, and covers the period from the Neolithic era to modern times. Among the exhibits are vases, excellent mosaics, figurines, statues, old coins, tools and weapons, inscriptions in Linear B and pottery from Cyprus imported into Crete during the Late Minoan period. There are also interesting Roman finds, including statues and mosaics.

Further south is the Cathedral. At the boundary with the New Town is the Public Market with its own characteristic colour and in the New Town itself the beautiful Public Gardens. Nearby are the Historical Archives of Crete which are the second largest in Greece in size and volume of documents. East of Chania is the upper class suburb of Chalepa and the home of Eleftherios Venizelos.

The Public Market, a building from the beginning of the 19th century.

Excursions from Chania

1. Akrotiri

6 km. *The tomb of the Venizelos family. An exceptional view of the town of Chania.*
9 km. *Junction which leads to the beach of Kalathas and the alluring sand beach at Stavros.*
14 km. *The road right leads to the airport.*

Above: The beach of Kalathas.
Below: The picturesque sand beaches of Stavros.

The interior entrance to the Monastery of Ayia Triada.

The Catholic Monastery of Gouvernetou.

16.5 km. The Monastery of Ayia Triada Zangarolon. *The church of the monastery, built in 1634, has a cruciform shape with a dome and an impressive facade. The monastery has a worthwhile museum.*

20.5 km. The Monastery of Our Lady of the Angels or Gouvernetou. *It is one of the oldest monasteries on Crete. It was most probably founded in the 11th century when the old main church was abandoned.*

Gouvernetou Monastery. Externally it has a fortress look with a strong Venetian influence in its architecture.

2. Mournies - Theriso

At interesting nearby place to visit is the village of **Mournies**, 4 km. from Chania. In the village is the house in which Venizelos was born; today it is a museum. Nearby is the famous Koukounara villa, a marvellous example of Venetian architecture, with fine gardens and fountains; the chief decorative motif is the winged lion of St Mark.

Theriso (16 km.). Theriso is a place of natural beauty which is also the starting-point for the ascent of the White Mountains. It was a landmark in the modern history of Crete.

The road runs through the impressive Theriso gorge, 6 km. in length and quite deep.

You leave the gorge and enter a densely-vegetated plain across which we can see the village of Theriso.

The village stands among the foothills of the White Mountains, at an altitude of 500 metres. Walks are organised to the highest peak of the Mountains, Pachnes, at a height of 2,452 metres.

The village acquired its greatest historical importance during the period of Cretan autonomy, with the revolt organised by Eleftherios Venizelos against the appointment by the Great Powers of Prince George as High Commissioner.

In 1905, Eleftherios Venizelos gathered his supporters there and proclaimed a revolution.

View of the historic village of Theriso, at the base of the White Mountains.

3. Omalos - Samaria Gorge (43 km.)

39 km. Omalos. A plateau at an altitude of 1,050 m., famed for its struggles for the liberation of Crete.

41 km. Left after 5 km. to the Kallergis refuge in the White Mountains from where the ascent to the highest peak Mt. Pachnes (2,453 m.) is made in about 7 hours.

43 km. Xyloskalos. From here you descend the celebrated Samaria Gorge. Before entering the gorge, should perhaps know that it is the longest in Europe, at a total length of 18 km., though the path through it is only 14 km. long. The width varies from 150 metres to 3 metres at its narrowest point, Portes ("Gates"). It has been declared a national park in an attempt to preserve its rare flora and fauna. Thanks to the wild and precipitous terrain, this is the only place in Crete where the native wild goat (agrimi or kri-kri) still lives. There are also many rare species of birds and all along the gorge there is a vast variety of herbs (including Origanum dictamnus, wild dittany) and flowers. For that reason it is forbidden to hunt, to light fires, to pick flowers and herbs or even spend the night in the gorge. In the winter, the gorge is impassable, and entrance is only permitted from May to October. The walk takes between six and eight hours, depending on one's walking abilities. Visitors should have with them strong shoes or boots and something to eat. There is no need to carry water, as there are frequent streams of cool, clear water. The time of sailing of the last boat from Ayia Roumeli, where the gorge ends, to Sfakia should also be ascertained.

Xyloskalos, at the top end of the gorge, is a narrow path with a wooden parapet to facilitate and protect those descending. As one goes down the path, the predominant feeling is one of awe; tall mountains tower to the right and left, while the gorge, seemingly endless, stretches out in front. The descent is four kilometres in length, and the landscape varies between plunging depths with high trees, springs of running water, and enormous rocks which look as if they are about to block the path.

After about 30 minutes there is a slight change in the view, as you pass the little chapel of St Nicholas, on your right, with tall cypresses. Now you are at the bottom of the gorge, and mountains whose peaks are close to 2,000 metres tower all around.

The gorge begins to open out and quite suddenly the water disappears underground.

Xyloskalos at the entrance to the gorge.

Here, half-way along the gorge, is the village of **Samaria**, uninhabited today because the wood-cutters and shepherds who used to live here were moved elsewhere when the area became a national park. The 14th century Byzantine church which survives has numerous icons and wall-paintings. It is dedicated to the Blessed ("Osia") Maria of Egypt, whose name was gradually corrupted to Sia Maria and thence to Samaria, giving the area its name. Samaria with its springs, is ideal for a rest and a picnic. In any case, you are halfway along the route.

Now the landscape changes. The gorge narrows, and the towering walls of rock come closer and closer. Shortly before the Gates, on the right, there is a little stream and a flat spot.

A little further along you come to the Gates themselves; a truly magnificent spectacle. The walls of the gorge are only three metres apart, towering to 600 metres on each side. And through the narrow opening the blue sea can be glimpsed in the distance. Now the path runs along a dry stream-bed, on round stones. Gradually it widens out again and you come to another deserted village, Ayia Roumeli. One further kilometre over the same stones brought down by the torrent in winter will bring you to the modern village of **Ayia Roumeli.**

The exit from the gorge is another of its pleasures. A swim in the Libyan Sea is the ideal end to a long walk; there is an excellent beach with coarse sand, black pebbles and a clear blue sea at **Ayia Roumeli.**

From there you can go on a ship of the line to Chora Sfakion. From Sfakia you will return to Chania.

The uninhabited hamlet of Samaria.

The "Gates" of the gorge.

4. Chrysoskalitissa
   Monastery-Elafonissi (78 km.)

At **37 km**. Turn left at **Kaloudiana**, on the road to Kastelli.

46 km. Topolia. A large village with the Byzantine churches of Ayios Ioannis, Ayia Paraskevi and Timios Stavros. A few kilometers beyond the village the **Topolia Ravine** begins. The road passes through a tunnel and arrives at the cave of Ayia Sophia. The chapel of **Ayia Sophia** is at its entrance.

57 km. Elos. The most beautiful of the villages in the area which are full of plane trees and chestnut trees (The "Chestnut Villages"). In October there is a **Chestnut Festival**.

61 km. Kefali. Village with a breathtaking view. Next to the school is the church of Ayios Athanasios, with wall paintings from 1393. Go past the right branch which leads to Sfinari and turn left.

73 km. Chrysoskalitissa Monastery. Down on the south-west extremity of Crete is a bay with enormous black rocks. On the highest one of them is perched the most beloved but also the most remote monastery.

Chrysoskalitissa Monastery.

78 km. Elafonissi. A small island replate with tranquility, colour and light. It has a lacey coastline and dazzling sand dunes with small cedar trees and lilies.

Elafonissi which is connected to dry land by a narrow passage 800 m. long.

5. Alikianos - Sougia (70 km.)

13 km. You leave the road to Omalos and go right.
14 km. Alikianos. In this village there are the ruins of the tower of the Venetian lord Damolino as well as the notable church of Ayios Georgios with wall paintings from the 14th cen.
70 km. Sougia. A tranquil little harbour with a lovely sand beach. In the village church is a mosaic with depictions of peacocks and deer.

6. Kandanos - Palaiochora (74 km.)

On the road to Kastelli you turn left at the 19th km. at Tavronitis.
27 km. Voukolies. A village with Byzantine churches which have wall paintings from the 15th century.
57 km. Kandanos. The capital of the Province of Selino. It was destroyed by the Germans because of its participation in the resistance. There are many eminent Byzantine churches in the surrounding villages, full of wall paintings.

The beach at Sougia.

74 km. Palaiochora. A market town with a spectacular sand beach and a warm sea. It is even suitable for swimming in winter.

The Palaiochora headland with its Venetian castle and the large sand beach to the west.

7. Kastelli - Falasarna (59 km.)

5.5 km. Galatas. Seaside village with a pristine sand beach. From May 20-25 various activities are held there connected with the Battle of Crete.

8 km. Ayia Marina. An extensive sand beach opposite the islet of **Ayioi Theodoroi.**

11 km. Platanias. Village with a sand beach beside a verdant hill.

17 km. Maleme. The area around the airport is known for the heroism of the Battle of Crete in 1941. There is also a German military cemetery here.

24 km. Right is **Kolymbari** on the edge of Chania with a beach. One kilometer north is the fortified **Gonia Monastery** or **Hodegitria** which today is the seat of the Orthodox Academy of Crete.

42 km. Kastelli Kissamos. It is built on the site of ancient Kissamos, the port of the ancient town of Polyrrenia.

Later, when it was occupied by the Romans, a new theater and Roman villas were built on top of the old town.
The town then passed to the Arabs and later the Venetians who built a small castle from which it took its new name. Kastelli is the capital of the Province of Kissamos, known for its superb wine. It has a harbour and is connected by ferry boat to Gytheio.
Gramvousa. This islet, has a famous Venetian castle. You can visit it by renting a motor boat at the castle.

53 km. Platanos. There is a road to this village which leads after 8 km. to the village of **Sfinari** with a splendid sand beach.

59 km. Falasarna. One of the most ravishing sand beaches on the Crete with emerald waters. It is impressive for its extent and charm. At the end of the sand beach is a steep and rocky hill on the top of which is the acropolis of ancient Falasarna.

Above: Ayia Marina and Platanos. Below: Kastelli Kissamos.   *The beach at Falasarna.*

8. Vrysses - Chora Sfakion - Anopoli (84 km.)

32 km. **Vryses.** *The main village in the area, with plentiful water.*

48 km. **Askyfou.** *A historic village at the beginning of a small but picturesque plateau of the same name. The large Imbros ravine begins after the village of* **Imbros.** *The landscape with its wild cypress trees is stunning.*

68 km. *A turn-off right leads after 12 km. to* Frangokastello *with a huge sand beach and a fortress built by the Venetians in 1371.*

70 km. **Chora Sfakion.** *Isolated on the difficult to reach coast of the Libyan sea, it was the center for the revolts to liberate the island. The old houses with their folk architecture that resembles Aegean architecture are built amphitheatrically around the harbour.*

From Sfakia you can take excursions on a small boat to Loutro, Ayia Roumeli, Sougia, Palaiochora *and the islet of* Gavdos.

82 km. **Anopoli.** *The village is built near the ancient town on a plateau 600 m. high. Next to the town is the striking gorge of Aradaina and opposite it a plateau. Iron bridges join the two plateaus.*

Frangokastello.

Chora Sfakion. On the slopes of a mountain, the road that goes to Anopoli can be seen.

9. Georgioupoli - Lake Kourna - Rethymno (61 km.)

6.5 km. Souda. This is the harbour that serves Chania. It is one of the biggest harbours in the Mediterranean and is at the same time a naval base. At the entrance to the bay is an islet of the same name on which the Venetians built a powerful fortress.

14.5 km. A turn-off left leads to the coastal settlements of **Kalami, Kalyves, Almyrida** and **Plaka** with lovely sand beaches.

38 km. A turn-off from the main route left leads to Georgioupoli and right to the only lake in Crete, **Lake Kourna.**

61 km. Rethymno.

Above: Lake Kourna in Crete.

Below: The large beach at Georgioupoli 9 km. long, protected from the northwest winds. The Armyros river, which has its source in lake Kourna, empties here.

THE PREFECTURE OF RETHYMNO

It borders to the west on the Prefecture of Chania and to the east on the Prefecture of Herakleion. The main mass of Mt. Psiloreitis (2,456 m.), the highest mountain in Crete, commands the prefecture to the east. There is found the Idaean Andron, the cave where, according to mythology, Zeus was raised.

The entire north coast of the prefecture is one vast sand beach, on the west end of which sits the pretty town of Rethymno. Near Rethymno is Arkadi, the historic monastery and on the south coast is another important monastery, Preveli. Next to it is the Kourtaliotiko Ravine with water running through it amid palm trees, one of the most beautiful landscapes in Crete.

Communications between the prefecture and the rest of Greece consist of a daily ferry sailing to Pireaus. There are also buses to Souda, where large car ferries serve the Chania-Piraeus line. From Chania airport at Akrotiri, Olympic Airways buses connect to Rethymno. In the summer, there are launch departures for Santorini and there are caique services from Ayia Galini to Matala in the Prefecture of Herakleio. Inside the prefecture, KTEL buses link the town with the villages and beaches.

Rethymno

Rethymno is the smallest of the three historic cities of Crete, with a population of 18,000. It is the capital of the prefecture by the same name and is the commercial and administrative centre for the surrounding area. It lies along the seashore approximately half-way between Chania and Herakleion. For that reason, the Venetian rulers of the eastern Mediterranean used it as a way-station and a refuge in time of trouble.

Rethymno is a most attractive little town which has never been damaged by earthquake and which has managed to retain both its oriental magic and its western grandeur. As one walks though its narrow Venetian alleyways with their little old houses with wooden covered balconies ("sachnisia"), their mosques and minarets, their Venetian mansions with magnificent flights of steps, coast of arms and Latin inscriptions, one has a strong sense of being carried back through time to the magic of another age.

Rethymno has a long tradition in scholarly and artistic matters, going back to Venetian times. Even then there were schools in Rethymno, teaching philosophy, mathematics and logic.

It stands on the site of a very ancient city called Rithymna. This city was autonomous and independent and it issued its own coins, which depicted Apollo.

Rethymno was at the height of its power and wealth in the Venetian period. At that time, indeed, it became a city and acquired its harbour, called Mandraki. In the 13th century the Venetians began fortifying the town, beginning with the wall to the west of the harbour.

Rethymno gradually grew into a major urban centre in which the Greek element was predominant in the population.

In the years 1540-1570 the Venetians strengthened the town's defences by building an outer wall. Only a short length of this has survived, together with the Great Gate. During this period, the town was attacked by various raiders and suffered damage.

In the years which followed, the fine fortress called the Fortezza was built on Palaiokastro hill. Among other buildings of the time were the Loggia, the Rimondi fountain, and the clock. Yet despite all the fortifications, the Turks captured it on 3 November 1646 after a siege of only 22 days. Under the Turks, Rethymno was the commercial port and administrative centre for the whole of western Crete. In the uprising of 1821 it suffered the same fate as the other Cretan towns, with massacres of the unarmed Christian population and looting. This did not prevent it from being a hotbed of resistance to the Turks. Between 1897 and 1909 it was occupied by the Russians, as part of the general occupation of Crete by the troops of the Great Powers.

The Venetian Rimondi Fountain.

Partial view of the Old Town of Rethymno.

The old town is built on a headland at the end of which is the small, but well-preserved, Venetian fortress of **Fortezza**.

At the entrance to it is the **Archaeological Museum**. The Museum collection contains finds from all over the prefecture, arranged in chronological order and covering all the periods in the history of the area.

There are figurines, tools, jewels and pottery from the Neolithic period, seal-stones, statuettes and votive offerings from the Minoan and Late Minoan periods, and interesting Egyptian finds — seals, scarabs and jewellery — which show how close were commercial contacts between western Crete and north Africa.

The Museum also contains exhibits from the Hellenistic, Roman, Byzantine and Venetian periods. East of the fortress is the picturesque little **Venetian harbour** and the commercial harbour.

Near this little harbour is the Rimondi fountain and the Venetian Loggia.

Further south is the church of St. Francis, the Turkish School, and the Great Gate, the central gate to the Venetian fortifications.

The harbour of Rethymno is connected to Piraeus by steamship.

Overall view of the Old Town of Rethymno.

Excursions from Rethymno

1. Arkadi Monastery *(22 km.)*

It is one of the most glorious monasteries in Greece while in Crete it is revered for the holocaust that happened there. In this monastery, on November 8, 1866, about a thousand people (monks, warriors and women and childern) led by the Abbot **Gavriel** preferred to die by blowing up the powder magazine than to fall into the hands of the Turks.

The monastery was founded during the time of the Venetian occupation. Its high walls are reminiscent of a fortress and the church, which has a baroque facade, is considered to be one of the most beautiful in Crete. It is double-aisled and dedicated to the Transfiguration of the Savior and Ayios Konstantinos and Ayia Eleni.

Facade of the monastery's main church.
The shelling of Arkadi - Folk painting.

2. Amari - Ayia Galini

You follow the road to Herakleion and at the 3rd km. turn right to Amari.

11 km. Prasses. A village with many Venetian houses, on the slopes of a verdant ravine.

29.5 km. Apostoloi. A village with old churches.

30 km. Ayia Foteini. A turn-off right leads after 4 km. to the village of **Merona** where there are noteworthy churches from the 14th and the 15th century with marvelous wall paintings and icons. At a distance of 7 km. from here is **Yerakari** at a height of 680 m. on the slopes of Mt. Kedros.

From Ayia Foteini a turn-off loft leads after 1 km. to the village of **Thronos**, where there are the ruins of ancient **Syvritos** and the church of Our Lady Throniani from the 11th century with remarkable mosaics and wall paintings. This is followed by the picturesque village of Kaloyerou.

35 km. Asomatos Monastery. It lies in a gorgeous setting. There is an Agricultural School at the monastery.

40 km. Amari. The capital of the like-named province with dense flora and beautiful Byzantine churches in the surrounding area. From Asomatos Monastery the road, after passing through the beautiful villages of Vizari, Fourfouras, Kouroutes and Apodoulou, meets the main road Rethymno - Ayia Galini - Herakleion.

Above: The Byzantine church of Ayia Paraskevi, one kilometre to the right before the Asomatos Monastery.

Below: The Amari valley with the villages of Thonos and Kalloyerou. Mt. Psiloreitis in back.

3. Spili - Ayia Galini

11 km. Armenoi
29 km. Spili. *The lovely main village of the area at the foot of Mt. Kedros; it is the capital of the Province of Ayios Vasileios, renowned for its abundant water and dense flora. There, in the square with the plane trees, the water runs from the 19 mouths of stone lions.*
55 km. Ayia Galini. *A notable tourist center built on the slopes of a hill which is above the harbour.*

Spili, the square with the fountains.

The quaint harbour of Ayia Galini.

4. Kourtaliotiko Ravine - Monastery of Preveli - Plakias (40 km.)

You follow the road that goes uphill toward the village of **Armenoi**.

19 km. Both roads lead to Plakias. The one straight ahead passes through the **Kourtaliotiko ravine** after 4 km.

21 km. Branch left leads to Spili and Ayia Galini.

29 km. Asomatos. A turn-off left leads after 4 km. to the **Lower Monastery of Preveli**. Another 3 km. and you arrive at the **Rear Monastery of Preveli** (St. John the Theologian) which is the main monastery. The monastery played an important role in the Cretan liberation struggles.

Two kilometers from the monastery the road ends at a path which leads to a river with palm trees which flows through the Kourtaliotiko ravine. It is worth the effort to go there and see at first hand the lake that has formed at its mouth.

36 km. From Asomatos you return to your main route to Plakias. At this point there is a branch which goes to Sfakia (42 km.) passing through the charming villages of **Myrthios, Selia, and Rodakino.**

40 km. Plakias. The ravishing sand beach and the beauty of the surrounding area have contributed to its spectacular development. A short distance from Plakias are the celebrated sand beaches **Damoni** (2 km.) and **Ammoudi** (3 km.).

Above: The main church of Preveli Monastery.

Below: Traversing the Kourtaliotiko ravine.

On pages 72-73: the river with the palm trees and the enchanting beach with the crystal-clear water at the exit from the Kourtaliotiko ravine (Lake Preveli).

5. Perama - Anoyeia - Idaean Andron
(76 km.)

You follow the road to Herakleion and at the 11th km., at Stavromenos, you turn right.

24 km. Perama. The capital of the Province of Mylopotamos. NE of Perama is the historic **Melidoni Cave** and S the village of **Margarites** with a pottery making tradition. Near the village are the ruins of the ancient town of **Eleftherna** which flourished from the Classical to the Roman period.

34 km. Mourtzana. Here you go right to the beautiful village of Garazo.

46 km. Axos. A picturesque village built below the ancient town of the same name. There are important Byzantine churches in Axos, such as Ayia Eirene from the 8th century and 12th century with incredible architecture and wall paintings and Ayios Ioannis from the 12th century.

South of Axos is the village of **Zoniana** with one of the loveliest caves in Crete, Sentoni or Sfentoni.

55 km. Anoyeia. A large, mountain village at a height of 740 m., which is a municipality and subject to the Province of Mylopotamos. It is near the border with the Prefecture of Herakleion. Anoyeia is well-known for its fabulous weaving with brilliant colours and the traditional Cretan designs. Its central square and lanes are full of these woven articles, which are on display for sale, giving the village a flavor all its own. Anoyeia, isolated on the north slopes of Mt. Psiloreitis, was a center of revolutionary activities against the Turks.

During World War II it was also distinguished as a focal point of the Greek resistance against the Germans.

Anoyeia was horribly punished for these activities. The Germans razed it to the ground in August 1944.

It was rebuilt and today is a noted tourist center. During the summer, parties are

Picturesque corner of Anoyeia.

organized in its tavernas at night, with Cretan dances.

76 km. Nida Plateau - Idaean Cave. At the end of the road and an altitude of 1,500 m. is the **Nida Plateau.**

Next to the road is a tourist pavilion so you can rest and enjoy the view of the plain which seems like a huge dry lake, surrounded by high mountains. A half a kilometer from the pavilion, on the rocky slopes of Psiloreitis, is the **Idaean Cave.** Magnificent, at the base of a gigantic rock, beneath the highest mountain on Crete; just the right place for a cave that mythology says was where Zeus, the father of all the gods, was raised.

From the Idaean Cave you can ascend to the highest peak of Mt. Idi, **Timios Stavros** (2,456 km.) in around 5 hours.

6. Rethymno - Herakleion (75 km.)

3 km. Perivolia. A splendid sand beach which has been touristically developed. A junction right for the national highway. The old road runs parallel to the new one, next to incredible sand beaches. The main ones are at *Adele* (5 km.) and *Stavromenos* (11 km.). From Stavromenos you follow the national road which goes through *Panormos* (22 km.) and then to Herakleion.

33 km. A turn-off from the main route left, leads after 2 km. to *Bali* a small but very pretty bay with a sand beach which has grown into a tourist center.

51 km. You now enter the Prefecture of Herakleion. From here a turn-off from the main route right leads after 3 km. to *Fodele* the village where the great painter *Domenicos Theotokopoulos (El Greco)* was born.

58 km. A turn-off left leads after 3 km. to the Bay of *Ayia Pelagia*, a modern tourist resort with a wonderful sand beach with crystalline water.

65 km. A turn-off left to *Ammoudara*, an extensive beach, west of Herakleion.

Above: Bali. Centre: Ayia Pelagia.
Below: The large beach of Ammoudara.

THE PREFECTURE
OF HERAKLEION

Here is Herakleion and the famous Minoan palaces of Knossos and Phaistos. In the southwest corner of the prefecture is the plain of Mesara, the largest and most fertile on the island. There, according to mythology, is where Zeus and Europa, the beautiful princess, settled after he abducted her from the court of King Phoenix. Minos was born from the union of Zeus and Europa.

The Prefecture of Herakleion is the largest prefecture in Crete and is where the administration of the island is centered and at the same time it has most of the important sights. North of Herakleion is the islet of Dia which is used as a sanctuary for the wild goat.

From the point of view of tourist facilities, the prefecture has a complete range of services. There are daily car-ferry sailings from Herakleion to Piraeus. Herakleion international airport is fully capable of meeting the considerable air traffic demands. There are domestic flights to Athens, Thessaloniki, Rhodes, Mykonos, Paros and Santorini. Inside the prefecture, there are town and long-distance (KTEL) bus services to all the villages, beaches and archaeological sites. In the summer, there are ferry sailings to the Cyclades, while cruise liners operating out of Venice link Herakleion to Limassol in Cyprus and Haifa in Israel. The large artifical harbour and the international airport of the town cover its communication needs which, however, are continually growing.

Herakleion

Herakleion is the largest town in Crete, the capital of the prefecture of Herakleion and the administrative capital of the entire island. All this was certainly contributed to by its geographical position. It lies in almost the middle of the north coast, just outside Knossos, has one of the most important museums in the world, and is close to the most interesting archaeological areas: Phaistos, Ayia Triada, Gortyn and Mallia.

Above right: The Venetian castle (Koules) at the harbour gates.

Below: View of the town of Herakleion.

Sunset at the old harbour of Herakleion.

According to Strabo, the modern city of Herakleion stands on the site of Herakleia, one of the ports of Knossos in antiquity.

The settlement continued to bear the name Herakleia throughout the Roman and first Byzantine periods, but its real history does not begin until 824, when it was captured by the Arabs. They fortified the town, built walls and dug a large moat round it: "handax", in Arabic, thus giving the town the name it bore down to the 19th century.

After a total of six unsuccessful campaigns, Candia was eventually retaken for Byzantium by Nicephorus Phocas in 961, marking the end of Arab dominion in Crete.

The Byzantines remained until 1204, when the Byzantine Empire was broken up by the Crusaders, and in their time the name Candia became internationally known and extended to the whole island: "Isola di Candia", it was called. In 1210, Candia was taken by the Venetians and became capital of the island. During the four centuries of Venetian rule, the marvellous walls were built.

The Venetians also built the harbour and adorned the town with magnificent public and private buildings, churches, fountains, etc., simultaneously making it an important commercial centre.

At this time, Candia flourished in the arts and letters under the influence of the Italian Renaissance, which was then in full bloom. After the fall of Constantinople in 1453, many scholars and artists took refuge in Candia, further strengthening learning there.

The Monastery of St. Catherine on Mt. Sinai set up a school in Candia, where theology, law and philosophy were taught.

The strength of the walls can be seen in the fact that although it took the Turks only two years to conquer the rest of Crete, Candia held out for 21 years of bitter siege (1648-1669).

After the departure of the Turks the town was given back its ancient name, Herakleion.

Herakleion consists of the **Old Town**, which is that part lying within the walls and the **New Town**, which spreads outside the walls.

The town of Herakleion is surrounded by the famous Venetian wall and one can only enter through certain gates in it. The town's center is the square with the lovely Venetian fountain of **Morosini**. Near there is the **Basilica of Ayios Markos**, built in 1239, the **Loggia** (both Venetian buildings) and the church of **Ayios Titos** which most pobably was built after the arrival of Nicephorus Phocas (961).

Other sights in Herakleion are the **Venetian harbour** and the **castle** with the winged lions in relief above the gate. There is the imposing **Cathedral of Ayios Minas** with the old Ayios Minas next to it. There are also **Ayia Aikaterini of Sinai**, which operates as a museum, where the paintings of the famous painter Michael Damaskinos are kept, the tomb of **Nikos Kazantzakis** on the Mertinengo Bastion of the walls and the **Historical and Ethnological Museum**.

Above: The Venetian fountain Bembo.
Centre: The "Koubes" cafe.
Below: The Morosini fountain in the centre of the town.

The Archaeological Museum

The **Archaeological Museum** is housed in a two-storey building in the neo-Classical style, constructed in 1937-40, and situated on the NW side of Eleftherias Square. The Museum is unique in that it contains only exhibits from Crete, covering the entire course of Cretan civilization from the Neolithic period to the end of the Graeco-Roman era.

The exhibits are organised and arranged in absolute chronological order, thus allowing visitors to follow the development of the island's great cultural tradition without any specialised knowledge of archaeology or even history. On the ground floor are the exhibits from the palaces at Knossos, Phaistos and Mallia, dating from the pre-Palatial, Early Palatial and Late Palatial periods and extending into the Greek and Geometric eras, and there is a special hall dedicated to sarcophagi.

On the upper floor are the frescoes, the Yamalakis collection and sculpture and smaller objects from the Greek and Graeco-Roman periods.

The jewellery, frescoes and exceptionally beautiful vases from the Minoan palaces are of the greatest artistic value. Among these exhibits, the faience figurine of the goddess with the snakes — a fertility symbol— is, perhaps, the most outstanding.

Above: Rhyton made of rock crystal. (Zakros, 1450 B.C.).
Left: Effigy of sanctuary with figurine of goddess.
Right: The "Lily Prince". Wall painting from the Palace of Knossos.

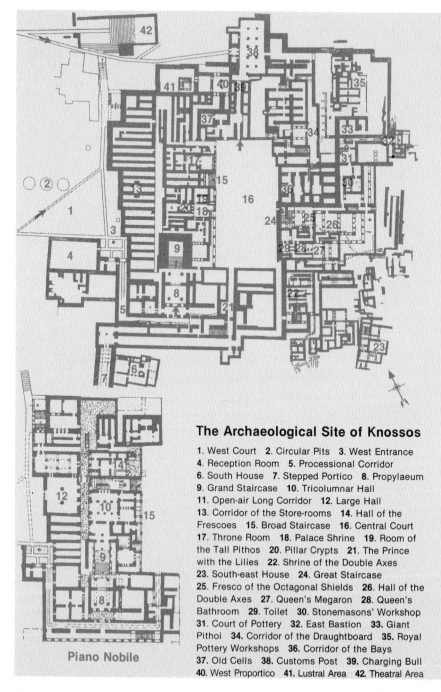

The Archaeological Site of Knossos

1. West Court **2.** Circular Pits **3.** West Entrance
4. Reception Room **5.** Processional Corridor
6. South House **7.** Stepped Portico **8.** Propylaeum
9. Grand Staircase **10.** Tricolumnar Hall
11. Open-air Long Corridor **12.** Large Hall
13. Corridor of the Store-rooms **14.** Hall of the
Frescoes **15.** Broad Staircase **16.** Central Court
17. Throne Room **18.** Palace Shrine **19.** Room of
the Tall Pithos **20.** Pillar Crypts **21.** The Prince
with the Lilies **22.** Shrine of the Double Axes
23. South-east House **24.** Great Staircase
25. Fresco of the Octagonal Shields **26.** Hall of the
Double Axes **27.** Queen's Megaron **28.** Queen's
Bathroom **29.** Toilet **30.** Stonemasons' Workshop
31. Court of Pottery **32.** East Bastion **33.** Giant
Pithoi **34.** Corridor of the Draughtboard **35.** Royal
Pottery Workshops **36.** Corridor of the Bays
37. Old Cells **38.** Customs Post **39.** Charging Bull
40. West Proportico **41.** Lustral Area **42.** Theatral Area

Piano Nobile

Excursions from Herakleion

1. Knossos (5.5 km.)

The most important archaeological site on Crete. It contains the ruins of the largest and most luxurious Minoan palace, built in the middle of a large town. The first palace was built around 2000 B.C. and destroyed around 1700 B.C. The second one was built immediately afterward, more magnificent than the first. This was also destroyed, around 1450 B.C., most likely by the terrible eruption of the volcano on Santorini. The excavations were carried out in 1900 by the English archaeologist Arthur Evans who then reconstructed certain sections of the ruins.

The visit to the Palace, which has an area of 22,000 sq. m., begins at the West Court. You will enter the palace through the West Propylaia and proceed down the Corridor of the Procession.

You turn left through the South Propylaia and climb up the monumental staircase to the upper floor (Piano Nobile) of the West Wing. You proceed first to the Tri-columnar Hall and then to the large hall and the sacred hall. You descend the small staircase to the corridor to the West Storerooms. You go to the Central Court to see in the South Corridor a copy of the wall painting of the "Prince with the Lilies". The original is in the Herakleion Museum. You visit the Tripartite Shrine which faces the

View of the Palace of Knossos.

Above: The "sacred bull's horns" at the south entrance.

The majestic "Throne Room".

Central Court and then the Lobby of the Stone Seat, the Pillar Crypts and the Temple Repositories where the snake goddesses were found.

From the Central Court you will then enter the Antechamber and the Throne Room with the famous throne of Minos, 4,000 years old, made of gypsum. Passing through the corridor of the North Entrance you arrive at the North Gate of the palace and the Hypostyle Hall or "Custom's House".

Left above: the grand staircase and the queeen's hall.

Below: The south propylaeum.

In the southwest end of the palace is the North Lustral Basin and outside the space, the Theater. To see the East Wing, you return to the corridor of the North Entrance and just before entering the Central Court turn left. You will be in the Corridor of the Draught-Board and the Magazines with the Giant Pithoi. Further south you will come upon the pottery workshop or the "School-room" and a stone-carver's workshop.

Going even further south you will arrive at the Royal Apartments. You descend the Grand Staircase and visit the Hall of the Double Axes where the King's Megaron, the Megaron and bathroom of the Queen and the Repositories are, where the famous ivory "Bull-Leaper" was found.

Finally, further south you will see the Shrine of the Double Axes, the Caravan Serai, the House of the High Priest, the Temple Tomb and the Royal Villa.

2. Gortyn - Phaistos - Matala

29.5 km. Ayia Varvara. *After a few kilometers you will face, from high up, the largest plain in Crete,* **Mesara.**

45.5 km. Gortyn. *For a length of 1 km. after Ayioi Deka there are the ruins of a large town scattered left and right of the road; during the Roman period this was the capital of Crete.*

The ruins of the basilica of St. Titus at Gortyn. The most important example from the first Byzantintine period.

There had been a small settlement on the site of Gortyn since the late Minoan period. But Gortyn became known later during the Archaic period and reached the high point of its glory in 69 B.C. when the Romans made it the capital of the Province of Crete and Cyrenaica and built many, majestic structures there, such as the **Praetorium** and the **Odeion**, next to which was found the famous Law-Code of Gortyn carved in stone blocks (see History, page 20).

The road left opposite the ruins of the basilica of **Ayios Titos**, *leads after 33 km. to the coast at* **Lendas**.

Ancient **Lebena** *was on the site of modern Lendas; it was built at the beginning of the Minoan period and flourished much later* during the Roman period when the inhabitants of Gortyn built a Temple of Asklepios there at the site of the therapeutic springs.

A gorgeous sand beach at Lendas is also suitable for winter swimming. Winter is so mild that it is said the swallows spend it there. From Lendas you can visit the remote **Monastery of Koudoumas** by caique.

On your return you follow the coast road which goes west to the marvelous sand beach of **Kales Limenes** where the Apostle Paul landed.

53.5 km. Moires. *A large transport, farming and commercial centre.*

60.5 km. *Left for Phaistos. The continuation of the road leads after 5 km. to* **Tymbaki** *and 3 km. more to* **Kokkinos Pyrgos,** *with a nice sand beach.*

62 km. Phaistos. *The second most important town in Minoan Crete with the luxurious palace of the mythical* **Radamanthys,** *the brother of Minos. The palace was built twice. The first time around 1900 B.C. during the so-called Old Palace Period. This was destroyed by an earthquake and in 1700 B.C. a new and more luxurious one was built during the New Palace Period. The second one was also destroyed, around 1450 B.C., probably by the eruption of the volcano on Santorini.*

The ruins of the second palace are what the visitor mainly sees today.

Unlike the Palace of Knossos, there have been no reconstructions or additions here.

The Palace of Phaistos.

The ruins were uncovered and left un-touched in the places they were found.

The architecture here is like that of Knossos with the palace being built around a rectangular, oblong and flagged Central Court which is oriented from north to south. Around the palace was the large Minoan town of Phaistos.

Just past Phaistos, a turn-off right leads after 3 km. to the ruins of a royal villa at **Ayia Triada** which was built in 1550 B.C. and was used as a summer palace.

Ayia Triada has given us a host of magnificent finds on display at the Herakleion Museum. Among them is the famous sacrophagus with the depictions of ceremonial libations.

68 km. Pitsidia. Near the village are the well-known sand beaches of Komos and Kalamaki.

73 km. Matala. A fishing village which just a few years ago was known as a hippy center and today has developed into a tourist resort.

The "Harvesters' Vase" from Ayia Triada.

Matala was the port of Phaistos and later Gortyn. There are caves carved out of limestone cliffs on the sheer side of the north hill.

Matala.

3. Tylissos - Anoyeia

Tylissos is known for the ruins of three Minoan villas (1700-1500 B.C.) which are located on the eastern side of the village next to a small grove of pine trees.

22 km. Sklavokambos. Ruins of a Minoan megaron.

36 km. Anoyeia. (see p. 74).

57 km. Idaean Cave. (see p. 74)

4. Zaros - Vrontisi Monastery - Kamares (55 km.)

You exit through the Chania Gate heading toward Phaistos.

29.5 km. Ayia Varvara. A lovely village at an altitude of 600 m. At the entrance, to the right, is a large stone outcropping with the church of Profitis Ilias on its summit, said to be the center of Crete.

From Ayia Varvara you turn right to Zaros.

39.5 km. Gergeri. A village built on a steep slope of Psiloreitis. Eighteen km. from here the marvelous forest of Rouva begins.

45.5 km. Zaros. A village with lush flora and abundant water. The old watermill still grinds wheat in the traditional manner. High up at the site Votomos, is a lovely artifical lake, at the entrance to a ravine.

50.5 km. A turn-off right leads after 1 km. to the Vrontisi Monastery, one of the most notable on Crete. It was built around 1400 and in the beginning was a monastic estate of the neighbouring Varsamonero Monastery. Wall paintings can be found in the church. The monastery's fountain from the 15th century is fabulous, with wonderful sculptures depicting Adam and Eve in Paradise.

The monastery began to flourish in 1500, when it appears the other one at Varsamonero was abandoned. It was a spiritual center and it is even said the great painter Michael Damaskinos lived and painted there.

52.5 km. Vorizia. Below left is the Varsamonero Monastery (1330-1426), one of the oldest monasteries in Crete and perhaps the most important in terms of the number and the quality of its wall paintings.

55 km. Kamares. A mountain village on the slopes of Psiloreitis at a height of 600 m. It is the starting point for the climb up to the Kamares Cave which was used as a place of worship during the Minoan period. The famous Kamares ware was found in this cave.

From Knossos a road meets, after 11 km., the road to Rethymno, Amari, Ayia Galini, and the plain of Mesara.

The famous fountain at the entrance to the Vrontisi Monastery.

5. Arkalochori - Ano Viannos - Arvi (84 km.)

At the 11th km. you go straight ahead.

33 km. Arkalochori. The main village in the area near which is a cave in which were discovered important Minoan finds. The old church of the Archangel Michael is in the village.

39 km. Junction left for **Kastelli Pediadas** and right for **Avli**. Go straight to Panayia.

55 km. A branch right goes to the plain of Mesara.

60 km. A turn-off right leads after 3 km. to **Chondros** and after 9 km. to the coast of Keratokambos and further west **Tsout-souros.**

66 km. Ano Viannos. A large village with dense flora, built high on the slopes of Mt. Dikte above a valley full of olive groves.

It is the capital of the province of the same name and the homeland of **Yiannis Kondylakis.**

In Ano Viannos you can visit the churches Ayia Pelagia and Ayios Georgios.

70 km. Turn right to Arvi. The view of the Libyan Sea from high up is truly exceptional.

84 km. Arvi. A charming, seaside village which took its name from a monastery of that name which was built on the slopes of the mountain. It is a tropical landscape and the entire plain is covered with banana trees.

Ano Viannos clinging to the slopes of Mt. Dikte.

6. Archanes - Archaeological sites

You follow the road to Knossos. At the 11th km. you turn right.

16 km. Epano Archanes. A market town amid vineyards, which produces the fine rozaki grapes. In the environs of Archanes are the

old churches of the Archangel Michael and Ayia Triada from the 14th century. Many of the areas near Archanes are of archaeological interest such as **Fournoi, Anemospilia, the peak sanctuary of Jucktas** and Vathypetro.

7. Herakleion - Ayios Nikolaos

From Eleftheria Square you follow the old road to Ayios Nikolaos up to **Phoinika.**

7.5 km. Karteros (ancient Amnissos). Here was the Minoan town of Amnissos, one of the three harbours of Knossos. Here is also the religious cave of Eileithyia, the patron goddess of child-birth.

13.5 km. Chani Kokkini. A dazzling coast of archaeological interest. Here are the ruins of the Minoan megaron of Nirou Chani from the New Palace Period.

15 km. Gournes. Seaside village.

20 km. Gouves (or Phoinikas). A tourist resort with a glorious sand beach.

29 km. Limenas Chersonisou. It is one of the largest tourist centres on Crete, owing to its fantastic sand beach and crystal-clear water. It flourished mainly during the Roman period.

Right: Views of Limena Chersonisou.
Below: View of the beach at Kokkini Chani.

34 km. Stalida. *Another beautiful beach. From here a turn-off right leads to the Lasithi Plateau (see page 103).*

37 km. Mallia. *An area of spectacular development. This was contributed to by two factors: the former Minoan palace which is 2 km. further on and the dazzling sand beach.*

39 km. The Palace of Mallia. *The third most important Minoan palace after Knossos and Phaistos. It has an area of 12,000 sq. m.*

It was built like the other Minoan palaces, around 1900 B.C., destroyed around 1700 B.C. and then built again more brilliant than before only to be finally abandoned in 1450 B.C. after a new calamity.

40 km. *A turn-off left leads after 3 km. to* **Epano Sisi** *from where you can go after 2 km. to* **Sisi** *with a nice sand beach.*

From Epano Sisi, turning right, you arrive after 6 km. at the village of Milatos was a historic cave and 2 km., further the shores of Milatos.

51 km. *A turn-off leads after 1 km. to* **Neapoli.** *A market town, it once was the capital of the prefecture of Lasithi. It has an* **Archaeological Museum.**

67 km. Ayios Nikolaos.

Above: Mallia, archaeological site.
Centre: The beautiful sand beach of Stalida.
Below: The small harbour at Sisi.

On opposite page:
Outside its archaeological interest,
Mallia also has a marvellous beach.

THE PREFECTURE OF LASITHI

On the Lasithi Plateau the spectacle of 10,000 windmills is unique. Here is the renowned Diktaean Cave, the cave where, according to mythology, Zeus was born.
On the northeast end of the prefecture is Vai, the fabulous sand beach embraced by date palms.
Communications by sea between the Prefecture and Piraeus are conducted through Herakleion. There are also sailings for Piraeus from Ayios Nikolaos and Siteia, via the Cyclades. Buses meet the flights into Herakleion airport. Siteia airport has flights for Rhodes, Karpathos and Kasos. Inside the prefecture itself, the villages are served by the town and long-distance KTEL buses.

The town of Ayios Nikolaos.

Ayios Nikolaos

Ayios Nikolaos has been the capital of the Prefecture of Lasithi since 1904. It stands at the northwestern extremity of the calm bay of Mirabelo, protected by mountains. It is an attractive modern town of some 8,000 inhabitants which, thanks to its exceptionally mild climate, verdant setting and calm sea, has become an international tourist resort. Its wind-free harbour is a meeting-place for countless pleasure craft, as well as the fishing-boats which are based there.

The little circular lake called Voulismeni in the centre of town is an undoubted attraction. A small zoo has been set up on the southwest side of the pretty lake. According to a myth, the goddess Athena used to come here to bathe.

The picturesque appearance of the town is accentuated by the two islets at the mouth of the quiet bay. The larger is called Ayioi Pantes; it has a church of the same name ("All Saints") and a lighthouse, and it is used as a breeding-ground for the Cretan ibex.

In antiquity, the site of Ayios Nikolaos was occupied by the port of Lato pros Kamara, which served the Doric city of Lato e Etera.

In the 3rd century B.C. this was a flourishing commercial port and an autonomous city which minted its own coins.

After that, it disappeared from history and was not mentioned again until the 13th century. In 1206 the Genoans built the fortress of Mirabelo on Kefali hill, where the prefecture building now stands, and it gave its name to the town and the whole bay. The fortress was flattened by an earthquake and later completely demolished by the Turks; today, no trace of it has survived.

In the 16th century, the Venetians gave the town its current name, which it took from the chapel of St Nicholas on the small promontory.

As a modern town, Ayios Nikolaos has no sights of historical interest. However, it does have an **Archaeological Museum** , founded in 1970 and located in a building at 68 Palaiologou St. The collection contains recent finds, most of them from eastern Crete.

The town has the Koundoureios Municipal Library, which contains 10,000 volumes.

Excursions
from Ayios Nikolaos

1. Elounda - Spinalonga -
   Plaka *(15.5 km.)*

9 km. *At the neck of the peninsula of Spinalonga is ancient Olous (2nd cent. B.C.-2nd century A.D.) whose ruins are today in the sea because the area subsided.*
10 km. Elounda. *A large tourist center. From here boats depart for a visit to the islet of* **Spinalonga** *with its Venetian fortress, the "Isle of Tears" as it has been dubbed because for 50 years this was the place of exile for lepers. You can also visit Spinalonga from Ayios Nikolaos.*
15.5 km. Plaka. *A seaside settlement with a lovely strand which has fine pebbles and crystalline water.*

The beautiful resort of Elounda with its up-to-date installations.

Views from the islet of Spinalonga on the north end of the Elounda headland.

Our Lady of Kera.

2. Kritsa - Ancient Lato

11 km. Panayia Kera. *One of the preeminent churches in Crete, both for its architecture and its marvelous wall paintings. It is triple-aisled and dedicated to Ayios Antonios, the Assumption and Ayia Anna.*

11.5 km. Kritsa. *One of the largest traditional villages on Crete with heightened tourist activity, known for its embroideries, knitwear and woven articles. In August there is a re-enactment of the famed Cretan wedding. **Ancient Lato** is 3,5 km. from Kritsa. **Lato e Etera**, as it is called to distinguish it from **Lato pros Kamara**, which was on the site of Ayios Nikolaos and was once a powerful town, built around the 7th century B.C.*

Embroideries and woven items at the village of Krista.

3. Lasithi Plateau -
Diktaean Andron (49.5 km.)

40 km. Mesa Lasithi. It is a lovely village on the plateau which you can reach at an altitude of 870 m.

From Mesa Lasithi a turn-off right leads to the **Kroustallenias Monastery** which was founded in 1540. At a distance of 3 km. from the monastery is **Tzermiado**, the largest village in the Province of Lasithi and its capital. Near the village are two notable archaeological sites. These are the Trapeza Cave and Kastellos hill. Both of them have furnished finds from the Neolithic, Early Minoan and Middle Minoan periods.

North of **Tzermiado**, there was a Late Minoan settlement at the rocky height **Karfi** (1,100 m.).

Windmill on the Lasithi plateau.

After visiting the pretty town of Neapoli, you begin to climb towards the plateau, which lies high in the Mt. Dikte range, at a height of 817-850 metres. The plateau, which occupies an area of 2,500 hectares, is surrounded by the high peaks of the range. Thanks to the geological composition of the ground, the plateau retains the rainfall and some 10,000 windmills raise the water from wells to irrigate the plain; apart from being picturesque, they also make the plain one of the most fertile parts of Crete.

Archaeological investigation has shown that the Lasithi Plateau was occupied as early as Neolithic times (Diktaean Cave). Settlements have been found at Karfi and Plati. In historical times, the area was part of the territory of the city-state of Lyttos. Under Byzantium, there was a large town at Avgoustis.

In 1263, however, the Venetians drove out all the inhabitants of the plateau, which had become a centre of resistance to their rule. They forbade any cultivation of the fields, on pain of death. And so for two whole centuries the plain lay fallow, its villages deserted and its fields waterlogged in winter. But when the Venetians had to deal with a shortage of wheat, they were compelled to allow the plateau to be farmed and inhabited again. They also helped to drain the area, digging the ditches which can still be seen today. Nonetheless, the plateau continued bo be a centre of revolt and a hiding-place for fugitives all through the period of Turkish rule. Today, the plateau is in the Province of

Lasithi; it has a total of 21 villages organised into 12 communities (administrative units). Thanks to its healthy climate, the fame of the Diktaean Cave and the spontaneous and unselfish hospitality of its people, it has become a major tourist attraction.

48 km. Psychro. *A village with tourist activity because of the nearby Diktaean Cave.*

49.5 km. Diktaean Andron (Cave). The road ends below the entrance to the cave. According to mythology, the cave is the place where Rhea gave birth to Zeus. The cave was a place of worship from the end of the Middle Minoan to the end of the Late Minoan period.

4. Ayios Nikolaos - Vasiliki - Ierapetra - Myrtos (51 km.)

12 km. *Bay of Voulisma (area of the shores of* **Kalo Chorio** *and Istros) Golden sands and clear waters.*

19 km. Gournia. *On the right side of the road, on the slopes of a hill, are the ruins of a Minoan town. The American archaeologist Boyd Hawes, who conducted the excavation, uncovered the foundations of an entire provincial Minoan town which flourished during the Late Minoan period (1600-1400 B.C.).*

20 km. Pacheia Ammos. *A tourist center and at the same time a communications hub. At 22 km. you turn right to Ierapetra.*

25 km. *A short turn-off right leads to the village of* **Vasiliki.** *Near there, in Early and Middle Minoan ruins, was found the famous pottery in the Vasiliki style with the long neck which bends at the end, making it look like a tea-pot.*

Ierapetra with its large beach.

36 km. Ierapetra. *The southernmost town in Greece with a ravishing beach on the Libyan Sea. Its name is derived from the ancient* **Ierapytna** *which in the 2nd century B.C. was one of the most important towns in Crete. Ierapetra is an active tourist center. It is only 14 km. from the north coast and 36 km. from Ayios Nikolaos. The area has a reputation for its resplendent sand beaches, its mild climate and abundant sunshine as well its early fruits and vegetables. It also has a small* **Archaeological Museum** *which contains finds from the Early Minoan to the Roman period. Like nearly all the large towns of Crete Ierapetra has a Venetian castle.* **Chrysi** *lies opposite Ierapetra.*

51 km. Myrtos. *A beautiful coastal village on a sandy beach. Near the village, the archaeological pick brought to light two Minoan settlements.*

The beach of Istros.   *Myrtos.*

5. Ayios Nikolaos - Siteia

20 km. Pacheia Ammos.

44 km. Sfaka. *From this village a turn-off right leads after 7 km. to the coast at Mochlos.*

63 km. Chamezi. *A village at an altitude of 380 m. Here at the end of September is a festival called "Kazanemata", the name given the traditional method of producing the renowned Cretan raki (tsikoudia).*

73 km. Siteia. *An attractive town with a harbour and a large sand beach. The capital of the easternmost province of Crete, it is built near the site of ancient* **Itea.** *The only ruins in the area are those of a* **Venetian castle** *to the east of the town. But the Province of Siteia is also one of the oldest centers of Minoan civilization as is shown by the finds at Mochlos, and the islets of Pseira and Ayios Nikolaos. You should not miss the* **Archaeological Museum** *and the small* **Folk Museum.**

6. Siteia - Kapsas Monastery - Ierapetra (59 km.)

From Siteia you follow the road to Piskoke-falo.

13 km. Four km. left is **Nea Praisos**. Ancient Praisos was an autonomous town which was inhabited from the Stone Age to the Venetian period.

32.5 km. A turn-off left to the **Monastery of Kapsas** next to the **Perivolakia ravine**, in front of a sandy shore. The monastery was probably built in the 15th century.

You return to the main route. Before it returns to Ierapetra the road passes along the endless sand beaches on the Libyan Sea with lovely settlements such as **Analipsi** *(34 km.)*, *Makrys Yialos, Koutsouras, Achlia, Ayia Fotia and Ayioi Saranta (55 km.)*
59 km. Ierapetra.

Kapsas Monastery.

The beach at Makrys Gialos.

7. Siteia - Vai - Kato Zakros

4 km. Ayia Fotia. *A splendid sand beach that has been developed.*

15 km. Toplou Monastery. It is a historic monastery on the northeast end of Crete, known for the struggle it waged against pirates and Turks. It was built in the 15th century, most probably on the ruins of an older monastery. It was a true fortress and even had a cannon. It has notable relics and wonderful icons.

23 km. A turn-off left leads after 1 km. to **Erimoupoli** (ancient Itanos).

24 km. Vai. The renowned palm forest with a great sand beach. It is a tropical landscape which is an exception in Greece. It receives a large number of visitors who come to see the rare landscape and enjoy its marvelous sea.

25 km. Return to Palaikastro.

33 km. Palaikastro. Large village with a wonderful sand beach.

South of Palaikastro are the ruins of a Minoan town and southeast the Minoan peak sanctuary of Petsofas which has yielded important finds.

50 km. Zakros. A verdant village with alluring alley ways. From here the road descends to the sea passing alongside the Ravine of the Dead.

58 km. Kato Zakros. A coastal settlement on a bay with pebbles and a crystal-clear sea.

This area became known for the famous Minoan palace which was discovered here by Professor N. Platon in 1961. The Palace of Zakros, the fourth of the great Minoan palaces, is very similar to the other three.

The difference is that the Palace of Zakros lay before a harbour which played an important role in the commercial exchanges with Egypt and other countries in the East.

The palace was destroyed the same year as the other large palaces, that is around 1450 B.C.

Above: Toplou Monastery.
Centre: Vai. Below: Zakros.
On opposite page: palm tree forest.

THE PREFECTURE OF CHANIA

HOW TO GET THERE

By airplane

Olympic: There are year round flights from Athens (west airport) to Souda (45'). The airport lies 15 km. northeast of Chania in the area of Akrotiri. Information: Olympic Arilines Athens, tel. (01) 9363363-5, Olympic Airlines Chania, tel. (0821) 57701-3, Chania Airport, tel. 63219, O.T.E. (Phone Company): 144.
Chania is connected to Thessaloniki by planes of Olympic Airlines.
Olympic Airlines Thessaloniki (031) 281880.
Charter flights connect the airport of Chania with many European cities during the summer months.
Air Greece: There are year round flights from Athens (east airport) to Souda (45'). Information: Air Greece Athens Agency, tel. 3255011-4, Airport tel. (01) 9600646-7.

By bus

There are KTEL buses from Thessaloniki to Chania. The buses are taken by ferry-boat from Piraeus to the harbour of Chania.
Information: KTEL Chania at Thessaloniki, tel. (031) 512121, OTE: 142.

By ferry-boat

There are a large number of boats from Piraeus to Souda in summer and somewhat fewer in winter.

The distance is 157 nautical miles (11 hours).
Information: Harbour-Master's Office Piraeus, tel. (01) 4226000, Piraeus Agency, tel. 4118611, Chania Agency, tel. 25656, O.T.E.: 142.
The harbour of Souda lies 7 km. east of Chania. It is connected by town buses. Information: Harbour-Master's Office of Chania, tel. (0821) 43052.
Kastelli Kissamos is connected by ferry-boat all year to Kythera (Ayia Pelagia), Antikythera, and the Peloponnese from Piraeus on the Piraeus - Peloponnese - Kastelli line.
Information: Harbour-Master's Office Kastelli, tel. (0822) 22024, Harbour Station at Kythera, tel. (0735) 31222, Harbour-Master's Office Gytheio, tel. (0733) 22262.

INTERNAL TRANSPORTATION

There are boats year round from Palaiochora and Sougia to Gavdos (4 hours). In the summer the boat also stops at Ayia Roumeli. Information: Harbour Station Palaiochora, tel. (0823) 41214. Throughout the year there is one boat a week from Chora Sfakion to Gavdos.
Information: Harbour Station Chora Sfakion, tel. (0825) 91292.
Chania is connected to Rethymno (58 km.) and Herakleion (137 km.) by KTEL buses. There are daily schedules, more frequent in summer. Information KTEL Chania, tel. (0821) 93052, 93306.

NDEX FOR THE PREFECTURE OF CHANIA

THE PREFECTURE OF RETHYMNO

HOW TO GET THERE

By airplane

Olympic: Rethymno is served by the airport at Akrotiri, Chania (Athens-Chania 45´). The 60 km. distance between Chania-Rethymno and back is covered by the Olympic Airlines bus. Information: O.A. Athens, tel. (01) 9363363-5, O.A. Rethymno, tel. (0831) 27353, 22257, O.A. Chania, tel. (0821) 57701, O.T.E. 144.

By ferry-boat

There are ferry-boats between Piraeus and Rethymno year round. Distance 160 nautical miles (Approximately 10 hours). Information: Harbour Master's Office Piraeus, tel. 4226000. Harbour Master's Office Rethymno, tel. (0831) 22276, Rethymno Agency, tel. 29221, O.T.E. 143. During the summer cruise ships run excursions to Santorini.

By bus

There are KTEL buses between Thessaloniki and Rethymno. The buses embark on a ferry-boat in Piraeus and transfer their passengers to Rethymno from the harbour at Souda, Chania. Information: KTEL Rethymno at Thessaloniki, tel. (031) 512121, O.T.E. 142.

INTERNAL TRANSPORT

There are many KTEL buses between Rethymno and Chania every day. Distance 60 km. (1 hour 10´). Information: Rethymno, tel. (0831) 22212. During the summer there are daily buses from Ayia Galini - Plakias - Rodakino to Chora Sfakion.

There are daily buses from Rethymno to Herakleion. Distance 79 km. (1 hour 30´ and 2 hours on the old road). There are also buses to Herakleion by way of Amari - Tymbaki - Moiries.

Information: KTEL Rethymno, tel. (0831) 22212 and Spili - Ayia Galini - Tymbaki. Information: KTEL Rethymno, tel. (0831) 22785.

DEX FOR THE PREFECTURE
F RETHYMNO

THE PREFECTURE OF HERAKLEION

HOW TO GET THERE

By airplane

Olympic: There are flights year round from Athens (west airport) to Herakleion (50'). The airport lies 5 km east of Herakleion.
Information: O.A. Athens, tel. (01) 9363363-5, O.A. Herakleion, tel. (081) 229191, Herakleion airport NIKOS KAZANTZAKIS tel. 245644, O.T.E. 144.

Charter flights connect Chania airport to many European towns in summer.

Air Greece: There are flights year round from Athens (east airport) to Herakleion (50'). Information: Agency Air Greece Athens, tel. 3255011-4, Airport, tel. 9600646-7.

Kretan: There are flights year round from Athens (east airport) to Herakleion (45'). Information: Kretan Airways, tel. 3311190-1, Kretan Herakleion, tel. (081) 342742-5.
Herakleion is connected to Thessaloniki, Rhodes, Mykonos and Santorini by Olympic Airlines. Information: O.A. Herakleion, tel. (081) 342742-5.

Herakleion is connected to Mykonos, Santorini, Rhodes and Thessaloniki by Air Greece. Information: Air Greece Herakleion, tel. (081) 330074-5, Herakleion airport, tel. (081) 330072, 330076.
Herakleion is connected to Thessaloniki by Kretan. Information: Kretan Herakleion, tel. (081) 342742-5.

By ferry-boat

There are a large number of boats from Piraeus to Herakleion in summer and somewhat fewer in winter.
Distance 174 nautical miles (12 hours).
Information: Harbour Master's Office Piraeus, tel. 4226000, Piraeus Agency, tel. 4177453, 4179822, O.T.E.: 143.
There are connections from Thessaloniki to Herakleion all year round. Distance 348 nautical miles (22 hours). Information: Harbour Master's Office Thessaloniki, tel. (031) 531504-5, O.T.E.: 143.
Herakleion is connected year round to the Dodecanese (Karpathos, Kasos, Rhodes) and the Cyclades (Irakleia, Naxos, Paros, Santorini) by ferry-boat from Piraeus and the Piraeus - Western Dodecanese line.
Herakleion is connected year round to Andros, Mykonos, Paros, Santorini, Syros, Tinos and Thessaloniki by ferry-boat from Thessaloniki and the Thessaloniki - Aegean islands - Herakleion line.

By bus:

There are KTEL buses from Thessaloniki to Herakleion. The buses are transported from the harbour of Piraeus to the harbour of Herakleion. Information: KTEL Herakleion, tel. (081) 245020, KTEL Herakleion in Thessaloniki, tel. (031) 525253, O.T.E.: 142.

INTERNAL TRANSPORTATION

There is a heavy schedule of KTEL buses with daily connections to Ayios Nikolaos (67 km.). Siteia (135 km.), Ierapetra (106 km.), Rethymno (79 km.) and Chania (137 km.), Information: tel. (081) 221765.

NDEX FOR THE PREFECTURE OF HERAKLEION

THE PREFECTURE OF LASITHI

HOW TO GET THERE

By airplane

Olympic: There are flights year round
between Athens (west airport) and
Siteia (1 hour 20').
Information: O.A. Athens, tel.
9363363-5, O.A. Siteia, tel. (0843)
22270, 22596, Siteia Airport, tel. 24666,
O.T.E.: 144.
Siteia is connected to Karpathos and
Kasos by Olympic Airlines from Athens.
Information: O.A. Siteia, tel. (0843)
22270, 22596.

By ferry-boat

There is a large number of boats from
Piraeus to Ayios Nikolaos and Siteia in
summer and somewhat fewer in winter.
Distance 200 nautical miles Ayios
Nikolaos, 206 nautical miles Siteia (12
hours Ayios Nikolaos and 12 hours 50'
Siteia). Information: Harbour Master's
Office Piraeus, tel. 4226000, Piraeus
Agency, tel. 4118611, O.T.E., 143.

Ayios Nikolaos and Siteia are
connected year round to the
Dodecanese (Karpathos, Kasos) and
the Cyclades (Milos) by ferry-boat from
Piraeus and the line Ayios Nikolaos -
Siteia - Kasos - Karpathos.
Siteia is connected year round to the
Dodecanese (Karpathos, Kasos,
Rhodes, Chalki) by ferry-boats of the
Aegean line. Information: Harbour
Master's Office Ayios Nikolaos, tel.
(0841) 22312, Harbour Master's Office
Siteia, tel. (0843) 22310.

By bus

There are KTEL buses from Thessaloniki to
Ayios Nikolaos. The bus is transported by
ferry-boat from Piraeus to Ayios Nikolaos,
Information: KTEL Lasithi in Thessaloniki,
tel. (031) 525253, O.T.E.: 142.

The prefecture is connected - by way of
Herakleion - with Rethymno and Chania by
KTEL Ayios Nikolaos, tel. (0841) 22234, Siteia,
tel. (0843) 22272, Ierapetra, tel. (0842) 28237.

DEX FOR THE PREFECTURE
F LASITHI

HOTELS OF CRETE

CHANIA

Agia Marina (0821)

Hotel	Class	Phone
ATRION	B	68636
SANTA MARINA	B	68570
AMALTHIA	C	68542
ARCHITECT'S VILLA II	C	68526
BELLA VISTA VILLAGE	C	68100
ELOTIS	C	681222
EROFILI	C	68529
MARINA SANDS	C	68691
SANTA MARINA II	C	68460
TA THODOROU	C	68510

Agia Roumeli (0821)

Hotel	Class	Phone
AGIA ROUMELI	B	25657

Almirida (0825)

Hotel	Class	Phone
ALMIRIDA BAY	B	31751

Daratsos (0821)

Hotel	Class	Phone
ALTHEA VILLAGE	B	31320
AGAPI	C	27410
LOTUS	C	31660
TALOS	C	28682

Elos (0822)

Hotel	Class	Phone
AGIOS DIKEOS	B	61275

Galatas (0821)

Hotel	Class	Phone
DAFNI	B	–
GRETA MARIA	C	51335
GIANNIS - ELENI	C	–
KORINNA	C	31767
VLACHOS	C	68526
VILLA ANASTASIA	C	31413
VILLA ARMONIA	C	22746

Georgioupoli (0825)

Hotel	Class	Phone
DROSSIA	B	61326
GORGONA	C	61341

Gerani (0821)

Hotel	Class	Phone
LENTARIS BEACH	C	–

Hania (0821)

Hotel	Class	Phone
AMFORA	A	42998
CAPTAIN VASSILIS	A	51122
CONTESSA	A	23966
KYDON	A	26190
PALAZZO	A	43255
PANDORA	A	43588
PANORAMA	A	31700
PORTO DEL COLOMBO	A	50975
AKALI MELATHRON	B	41000
AKROTIRI	B	24669
ARKADI	B	40181
ARGYRO	B	55019
ARIADNI	B	31484
ARTEMIS	B	–
DONA	B	21772
DOMENICO	B	55019
EL GRECO	B	22411
FALIRO	B	41905
GHIANNIS	B	–
ILIANTHOS	B	20828
LISSOS	B	24671
MONTE VARDIA	B	40872
NOSTOS	B	54833
NOTOS	B	54278
PASIPHAE	B	–
PORTO VENEZIANO	B	29311
SAMARIA	B	51551
XENIA	B	224561
AFRODITI	C	57602
AMPHITRITI	C	56470
APTERA BEACH	C	22636
ARIS	C	–
ASTOR	C	55557
CANDIA	C	26660
CANEA	C	24673
DICTYNNA	C	21101
HELLINIS	C	28070
IRENE	C	54203
KRITI	C	21881
KYDONIA	C	57561
LATO	C	56944
LUCIA	C	21821
MANOS	C	29493
MARY POPPINS	C	26357
OMALOS	C	57171
PHILIP	C	–
PLAZA	C	22540
THEOFILOS	C	53294
ZEPOS	C	44921

Kalathas (0821)

Hotel	Class	Phone
LENA AKTI	B	–
APOLLO VILLA APTS	C	–
ARION	C	57388
SUNRISE	C	64214
TZANAKAKI BEACH	C	64363

Kamissiana

Hotel	Class	Phone
DOM'S STUDIOS	C	22375

Kato Stalos (0821)

Hotel	Class	Phone
ALCYON	B	68021
ARCHITECTS' VILLAS	C	68526
DOLFIN	C	68507
KATO STALOS	C	68120
PAVLAKIS BEACH	C	68309

Kissamos (0822)

Hotel	Class	Phone
HELENA BEACH	B	23300
CASTLE	C	22140
DIMITRIS-CHRYSSANI	C	23390
KISSAMOS	C	22086
PELI	C	22343

Kolymbari (0824)

Hotel	Class	Phone
ARION	B	22440
AEOLOS	C	22203
AKROTIRI IRINIS-FILIAS	C	22485

Korakies (0821)

Hotel	Class	Phone
CORAKIES VILLAGE	B	64584

Kounoupidiana (0821)

Hotel	Class	Phone
PYRGOS	B	64431
PHILIPPOS	C	64231

Kourna (Paralia) (0825)

Hotel	Class	Phone
HAPPY DAYS BEACH	C	61201
KAVROS BEACH	C	–
MANOS BEACH	C	61221
ORFEAS BEACH	C	61218

Maleme (0821)

Hotel	Class	Phone
CRETE CHANDRIS	A	62221

Paleochora (0823)

Hotel	Class	Phone
AGHAS	B	41525
ARIS	B	41502
ELIROS	B	41348
ELMAN (Pahia Amos)	B	41412
LISSOS	C	41266
POLYDOROS	C	41068
REA	C	41307

Platanias (0821)

Hotel	Class	Phone
FILOXENIA	B	68502
GERANIOTIS BEACH	B	68681
VILLA PLATANIAS	B	48333
AGAPI	C	–
ELENI	C	68218

Rapaniana (0824)

Hotel	Class	Phone
KASTRO	C	4858
OLYMPIC	C	2248

Sfakia (0825)

Hotel	Class	Phone
XENIA	B	9120

Sougia (0823)

Hotel	Class	Phone
PIKILASSOS	B	5124

Tavronitis (0824)

Hotel	Class	Phone
LYKASTI	C	2216

Trahilos (0822)

Hotel	Class	Phone
VAI	C	2279

RETHYMNO

Agia Galini (0832)

Hotel	Class	Phone
ANDROMEDA	B	9126
REA	B	9139
STELLA	B	9135
ACROPOLIS	C	9123
ADONIS	C	9133
ADONIS II	C	9133
ARIADNI	C	9138
ASTORIA	C	9125
ATHINA	C	9133
CANDIA	C	9120
DEDALOS	C	9121
EL GRECO	C	–
GALINI MARE	C	9135
GHIOMA	C	9119
IRO	C	9116
MIRAMARE	C	9122
PETRA	C	9115
PHAESTOS	C	9122
SELENA	C	9127
SOULIA	C	9130

Bali (0834)

Hotel	Class	Phone
BALI BEACH	B	9421

Missiria (0831)

Hotel	Class	Phone
ANNA	B	2259
DOMENIKA	B	–
MAY	B	2174
ODISSIA BEACH	C	2787
SEVEN BROTHERS	C	2563
VENUS	C	2563

Panormos (0834)

Hotel	Class	Phone
KIRKI	B	5125
PANORMO BEACH	C	5132

Perivolia (0831)

Hotel	Class	Phone
OASSIS	A	4470
ELTINA	C	2238
KANTARAS	C	2559
PLAZA	C	2979
ZANTINA BEACH	C	2486

Plakias (0832)

Hotel	Class	Phone
CALYPSO		
CRETIAN VILLAGE	A	3129
LAMON	B	3120
NEOS ALIANTHOS	B	3128
ALIANTHOS	B	3128
LIVYKON	C	3121
LOFOS	C	3142
MYRTIS	C	3143
PLAKIAS BAY	C	3125
SOPHIA BEACH	C	3125

Platanes (0831)

Hotel	Class	Phone
BUENO	B	2555
NEFELI	B	2132
SANDY BEACH	B	2699

STETHALI	B	25551
AXOS	C	23513
GALEANA	C	29553
TRYFON	C	24771

Rethimno (0831)

CRETA STAR	A	21896
EL GRECO	A	71102
RETHYMNO BAY	A	27512
RETHYMNO MARE	A	(0834) 93265
RITHIMNA BEACH (Adele)	A	29491
THEARTEMIS PALACE	A	21991
VYZANTIO	A	—
ADELE BEACH BUNGALOWS	B	71047
AMNISSOS	B	71502
BELVEDERE	B	26898
BRASCOS	B	23721
DIAS (Adele)	B	71017
ELEONORA	B	25121
ELINA HOLIDAYS	B	27395
EVA BAY (Adele)	B	71248
FILOXENIA	B	21345
GORTYNA	B	93381
DAEON	B	28667
IASON	B	27196
IO-AN	B	24241
KRITI BEACH	B	27401
Kalithea)	B	21326
LEON	B	26197
LIBERTY	B	—
MINOS (Kalithea)	B	24173
NIKA (Koube)	B	—
OASSIS	B	93274
OLYMPIC	B	24761
ORION (Kambos Adele)	B	71471
RETHEMNIOTIKO SPITI	B	23923
SKALETA BEACH	B	93244
XENIA	B	29111
ZANIA	B	28169
ZORBAS BEACH	B	28540
ARMONIA	C	23905
ARSINIA	C	71283
ASTALI	C	24721
GOLDEN BEACH (Adele)	C	71012
GOLDEN SUN (Adele)	C	71284
GREEN	C	22225
ONIA	C	22902
LIOS	C	21672
KATERINA BEACH (Adele)	C	71270
KOUKAKIS	C	—
KYMA BEACH	C	21503
LEFTERIS	C	23803
LOGGETA	C	27846
MARITA (Mastambas)	C	26991
MARKOS	C	—
MERLIN	C	—
MIRAMARE BEACH	C	24118
MOUSTAKIS	C	—
NIKI	C	71038
PARK	C	29958
PAVLOS (Stavromenos)	C	71304
RINA (Adele)	C	71013
SEASIDE INN (Xirokamaro)	C	71503
STERIS BEACH (Kalithea)	C	28303
VALARI	C	22236
VASSIANI	C	—
VENETIA	C	25092
VILLA ADELE (Adele)	C	71271

Violi Haraki

AMBELI	C	21233

HERAKLEION

Agia Pelagia (081)

CAPSIS BEACH	A	811112
PENISULA	A	811313
MONONAFTIS	B	—
PANORAMA	B	811002
PERLA	B	289406
STELIOS	B	—
ANASTASSAKI	C	—
THALIA	C	—
VILLA TSOLAKI	C	811032

Amnissos (081)

MINOA PALACE	A	227802

Amoudara (081)

AGAPI BEACH	A	250502
DOLPHIN BAY	A	821276
AGAPI VILLAGE	B	250524
LAMBI	B	821124
MARILENA	B	254312
AGIA ELENI	C	—
AGHIOS BAY	C	—
GERANI	C	—
MINOAS	C	821557
TSANGARAKIS BEACH	C	251768
VIOLETTA	C	250773

Arvi (0895)

ARIADNI	C	71300

Gournes (0897)

ERATO	B	761277
AMARYLLIS	C	—

Gouves (0897)

CRETA SUN	A	243794
MARINA	A	41361
APHRODITE BEACH	B	41102
APOLLO	B	41271
ASTIR BEACH	B	41141
BYRON	B	41130
CHRISTI APTS	B	—
MARIYANNA	B	—
CAPYPSO HOLIDAYS	C	41390
DESPO	C	41353
DIOSCOURI	C	—
EDERI	C	41204
GOUVES SEA	c	41401
KOUROS	C	41389
LAVRIS	C	41101
MANIA	C	—
MON REPOS	C	41280
SERENITE	C	—
SONIA	C	41368
STUDIOS LIDA	C	41456

Hani Kokini (081)

ARINA SAND	A	761113
KNOSSOS BEACH	A	761204
THEMIS BEACH	A	761412
PRIMA	B	761109
XENIA ILIOS	B	—
AKTI	C	761260
ARMILIDES	C	761256
DANAE	C	761375
IRIS	C	—
KAMARI	C	761340
SOTIRIOU	C	—
VILLES MARO-DIMITRIS	C	—

Iraklio (081)

ASTORIA	A	286462
ATLANTIS	A	229103
CRETA BEACH	A	252302
GALAXY	A	238812

XENIA	A	284000
ANNA-BELLA	B	289728
ARES	B	280646
ATRION	B	242830
DIAS	B	223950
ESPERIA	B	288512
ILAIRA	B	227103
KASTRO	B	285020
KRETA	B	282238
KRIS	B	223211
MEDITERRANEAN	B	289331
PETRA	B	229912
XENON GEORGIADES	B	284808
APOLLON	C	250025
ASTERION	C	227913
ATHINAIKON	C	229312
ATLAS	C	288989
BLUE SKY	C	254612
CASTELLO	C	251234
DAEDALOS	C	224391
DOMENICO	C	228703
EL GRECO	C	281071
EVANS	C	223928
GORGONA	C	821180
GORTIS	C	255820
GLORIA	C	288223
GRABELLES	C	241205
HERACLEION	C	281881
IRENE	C	226561
KNOSSOS	C	283247
KRONOS	C	282240
LATO	C	225001
MARIN	C	220737
METROPOLE	C	244280
MIRABELLO	C	285052
OLYMBIC	C	288861
SANTA ELENA	C	251770
SELENA	C	226377
SOFIA	C	224971

Karteros (081)

AMNISSOS	B	281332
KARTEROS	B	228802
MOTEL XENIA	B	281841
XENIOS DIAS	C	285694

Kokinos Pirgos (0892)

FILIPPOS	B	52002
LIBYAN SEA	B	51621
TA ADELFIA	C	51462
MARY-ELEN	C	51268

Krassi Pediadas

PETALO	B	—

Limenas Hersonissou (0897)

CRETA MARIS	L	22115
BELVEDERE	A	22010
CRETAN VILLAGE	A	22295
EAST APARTMENTS	A	22850
GALAXY VILLAS	A	22910
KASTRI VILLAGE	A	22102
KING MINOS PALACE	A	22781
LYTROS	A	22575
NANA BEACH	A	22706
ORION	A	—
PEFANA VILLAGE	A	22411
WEST APARTMENTS	A	22850
ADONIS	B	22141
ALEKA - NANCIA	B	—
ANGELOS	B	22258
ASSITES	B	22968
CRYSSI AMOUDIA	B	22971
DEDALOS VILLAGE	B	22515
DENISE	B	—

Name	Class	No.
DIANA	B	–
GLAROS	B	22106
HARIS	B	22346
HERSONISSOS	B	22588
HERSONISSOS MARIS	B	22354
IDILIO	B	–
IOKASTI	B	22607
KOUTOULOUFARI APTS	B	22688
LENA - MARY	B	22907
MARAGAKIS	B	22405
MARIA	B	22580
MASTORAKIS	B	22965
NORA	B	22751
OCEANIS	B	22671
PARMAKELIS	B	–
PANORAMA	B	–
PHAEDRA HERSONISSOU	B	–
PORTO GRECO	B	–
SERGIOS	B	22583
SILVA MARIS	B	22850
STELLA	B	22650
STELLA VILLAGE	B	–
TRADITIONAL HOUSE	B	–
VENUS MELENA	B	22892
VILLES ESPERIDES	B	22322
VIRGINIA	B	22466
VOULA	B	22097
VRITO	B	22401
ADAMAKIS	C	22447
AGRABELLA	C	–
ALBA	C	–
ALBATROS	C	22644
ALEKOS	C	22110
ALONI	C	22562
ANGELOS VILLAGES	C	–
ANNA	C	22753
ANNIRIN	C	–
ANNITA	C	–
ANTINOOS	C	–
ARIADNE	C	22312
ARMAVA	C	22544
ASPA	C	–
ASPETIS	C	22062
AVERINOS	C	22994
AVRA	C	22203
BIZANTIUM	C	22940
BLUE SKY	C	22208
CHARALAMBAKIS-GEORGALIS	C	–
DASSIA	C	–
DIKTINA	C	22648
DIMICO	C	22697
DIMITRA	C	22225
EVA	C	22090
FILIPPAKIS	C	22165
FILOXENIA	C	22835
FLISVOS	C	22006
FLORAL	C	23004
GALINI	C	22207
GOLDEN BEACH	C	22391
HELEANA	C	22830
HELENA	C	22226
HERCULES	C	22527
ILIOS	C	22700
IRO	C	22136
KATERINA	C	22304
MAISTRALI	C	22133
MARIANNA	C	22709
MARGARITA	C	–
MARIE - GEORGE	C	22991
MARIETA	C	–
MARIETA II	C	–
MARINA	C	22041

Name	Class	No.
MARITA	C	22310
MARIE-CHRISTINE	C	22537
MELINE	C	–
MELPO	C	22646
MEMORY	C	22497
MINAS	C	–
MINI HOME	C	–
MIRAMARE	C	22796
NANCY	C	22212
NIKI	C	22379
OASSIS	C	22932
PALMERA BEACH	C	22481
PELA - MARIA	C	22195
PERAKIS	C	22968
PERIGHIALI	C	–
PISKOPIANO	C	22726
PLAZA	C	22760
PSARROS	C	22534
REA	C	22357
REGINA	C	22007
SOFI	C	22557
STELIOS	C	22046
STELLA PARADISSOS	C	22759
TAXIARCHIS	C	–
THALIA	C	22590
THEODORA	C	23158
VASSO	C	22047
VELISSARIOS	C	22946
VILLA IPPOKAMBI	C	22316
VILLA MARGARITA	C	22610
YANNADAKIS	C	22937
ZORBAS	C	22075

Linoperamata (081)

Name	Class	No.
APOLLONIA BEACH	A	821602
ZEUS BEACH	A	821503

Malia (0897)

Name	Class	No.
IKAROS VILLAGE	A	31267
KERNOS BEACH	A	31421
MALIA BEACH	A	31210
SIRENS BEACH	A	31321
ALEXANDER BEACH	B	31568
ANASTASSIA	B	31180
ARIADNE	B	31592
CALYPSO	B	31363
COSTAS	B	31485
CLEO	B	31112
GRAMMATIKAKI	B	31366
KOSMIMA MALLION	B	–
MOONLIGHT	B	–
PHAEDRA BEACH	B	31560
SUNSHINE	B	31401
ATLIS	C	31217
AMVROSSIA	C	31378
ARTEMIS	C	31583
DIONYSSOS	C	31475
EFI	C	31640
ELKOMI	C	31595
FLORELLA	C	31664
FRIXOS	C	31941
GHIANNIS - MARIA	C	31313
HELEN	C	31545
HERMES	C	31788
ILMA	C	–
MALIA HOLIDAYS	C	31206
MALIA MARE	C	–
MALIA STUDIOS	C	–
MINOA	C	31465
MINOIKOS ILIOS	C	31106
MISTRAL	C	31934
NEON	C	31997
SOFOKLES BEACH	C	31348
STERLING	C	31563

Name	Class	No.
SUN BEACH	C	3155
VILLA ROZA	C	–
WINDMILL	C	3164

Matala (0892)

Name	Class	No.
SUN	B	–
BAMBOO SANDS	C	4237
EVA - MARINA	C	4212
FRANGISKOS	C	4238
MATALA BAY	C	4210
PRINGIPISSA EVROPI	C	421

Paleokastro (081)

Name	Class	No.
THEA	B	–
ROGDIA	C	82137

Piskopiano (0897)

Name	Class	No.
KALIMERA	B	–
PANORAMA	B	2250
STELVA II	B	2289
STELVA VILLES	B	2289
VILLES MIKA	B	2298
ANNA - MARIA	C	2225
EDELWEIS	C	2263
KORIFI I	C	–
KORIFI II	C	–

Poros (081)

Name	Class	No.
PASIPHAE	C	28313
POSEIDON	C	28585
PRINCE	C	28710
VINES	C	28575

Servili Tilissou

Name	Class	No.
AROLITHOS	A	–

Stalida (0897)

Name	Class	No.
ANTHOUSSA BEACH	A	3138
CRETA SOLARIS	A	3149
PRIMAVERA	A	3159
ALKYONIDES	B	3155
AMAZONES VILLAS	B	3148
ANATOLI	B	–
BLUE SEA	B	3137
CACTUS BEACH	B	3131
DIAMOND BEACH	B	–
ELVIRA	B	3163
KORINA		31957
PALM BEACH	B	3166
PANORAMA STALIDOS	B	3195
PENELOPE	B	3137
SMARAGDINE BEACH	B	3158
SUNNY BEACH	B	3158
THISVI	B	3196
ZEPHYROS BEACH	B	3156
ALEX	C	6132
ARMINDA	C	2248
CAPTAIN'S VILLA	C	3159
ELECTRA	C	–
HELIOTROPE	C	3151
L'AMOUR	C	3161
LATANIA	C	3155
NIKI	C	–
PELARGOS	C	6132
VILLA ANNA	C	3150
VILLA MARIA	C	3145
VILLA RITSA		31492

Timbaki (0892)

Name	Class	No.
AGIOS GEORGIOS	C	5167

Vori (0892)

Name	Class	No.
AGIOS GEORGIOS	C	5167

Vori

Name	Class	No.
PATRIKO	B	–

Zaros (0894)

Name	Class	No.
IDI	C	3130

ISLETS AROUND CRETE

THE PREFECTURE OF CHANIA

GRAMVOUSA. *This islet, on the northw*
side of Chania with its sheer coastline, ha:
famous Venetian castle. You can visit it
renting a motor boat at Kastelli. NW
Gramvousa is Agria Gramvousa *and SW of t*
Pontikonisi.

GAVDOS. *This is the island of Calypso or*
many believe and at the same time t
southernmost settlement in Europe. It is
miles from Crete and around 150 miles from i
coast of Africa. Its few inhabitants are scatte
among its four villages. There is a superb sa
beach at Sarakiniko, 30´ on foot from t
harbour. You can go to Gavdos by caique fr
Palaiochora or Chora Sfakion. South of Gavc
is Gavdopoula.

Thodorou. . . . . *N Ayia Mari*
Souda, Palaiosouda. . . . . . . *Souda B*
Elafonissi. . . . . *NW of Cre*
Artemis. . . . . *SE of Elafoni*
Koursaroi, Prasonisi. . . . . . *S Falasar*
Petalida. . . . . *E Falasar*
Lazaretto. . . . . *E Char*
Schistonisi. . . . . *S Palaiocho*

THE PREFECTURE OF RETHYMN

Diapori. . . . . *E B*
Prasonisi, Paximadia. . . . . *SW Ayia Gal*

THE PREFECTURE OF HERAKLEIO

Dia, Paximadia. . . . . *N Herakleic*
Glaronisi. . . . . *NW L*
Megalonisi, Mikronisi. . . . . *S Kali Lime*
Thetis. . . . . *E Treis Ekklisi*

THE PREFECTURE OF LASITHI

CHRYSI. *It is also called Gaidouronisi. It is*
islet with dazzling white sand beaches a
forests of small cedar. It lies opposite lerape
and is about one hour by caique. East of it
Mikronisi.

Spinalonga. . . . . *N Eloun*
Kolokythia. . . . . *E Eloun*
Ayioi Pantes. . . . . . . *NE Ayios Nikolac*
Konida. . . . . *N Pacheia Amm*
Pseira. . . . . *W Mochlc*
Ayios Nikolaos. . . . . *N Mochlc*

DIONYSIADES:

Yianysada. . . . . *NE Site*
Dragonada. . . . . *NE Site*
Paximada. . . . . *NE Site*
Keramidi. . . . . *NE Site*
Elasa. . . . . *E Va*
Grandes. . . . . *E Palaiokast*
Koufonisi. . . . . *SE Cre*
Strongylo, Makroulo. . . . . . *N Koufon*
Trachilos. . . . . *S Koufon*
Prasonisi, Kimo, Kavaloi. . . . . *SE Cre*

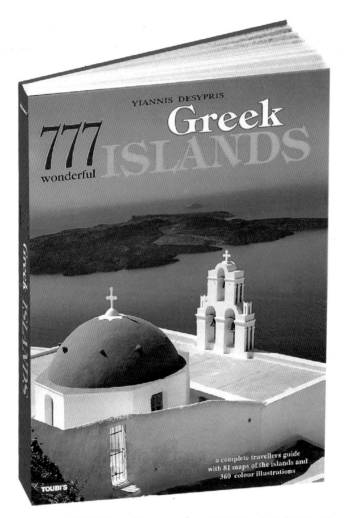

777 Greek ISLANDS

Many years in preparation, now completed in 1994. A unique edition which treats 777 beautiful Greek islands from the 9,500 islands and rocky outcroppings of the Greek Archipelago.

360 colour illustrations, 81 maps of the islands, format: 17 × 24, pages: 272

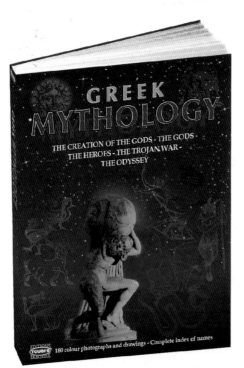

GREEK MYTHOLOGY

This special edition has been designed to present the main Greek myths.
A work of considerable scope, written in a simple and expressive language, it is accompanied by 180 photographs and excerpts from ancient Greek literature.

Format: 17 × 24 cm, Pages: 176
Photographs: 180

THE GREEK COOKERY BOOK

You can visit culinary Greece through one of our "THE GREEK COOKERY BOOK" latest publications prepared especially for you. In this book you will find representative Greek dishes, traditional recipes and specialities for official holidays, with easy instructions for their preparation numerous and lavish illustrations as well as the calories each dish contains.

Format: 17 × 24 cm, Pages: 176
Photographs: 150